on track ...

Renaissance

every album, every song

David Detmer

sonicbondpublishing.com

Sonicbond Publishing Limited

www.sonicbondpublishing.co.uk

Email: info@sonicbondpublishing.co.uk

First Published in the United Kingdom 2021

First Published in the United States 2021

British Library Cataloguing in Publication Data:

A Catalogue record for this book is available from the British Library

ISBN 978-1-78952-062-0

Typeset in ITC Garamond & ITC Avant Garde

Printed and bound in England

Graphic design and typesetting: Full Moon Media

Acknowledgements

My biggest thanks go to my friend, John Wachala, a brilliant musician and music teacher, who discussed several Renaissance tracks with me, often noticing crucial details that I had missed, and also correcting some of my errors. If you find this book to be of value, much of the credit should go to John.

Special thanks also go to Kerri and Arlo, for all the love, fun, and inspiration they bring to my life.

Thanks to Stephen Lambe, and all the folks at Sonicbond, for producing this book, and for giving me the opportunity to write it.

Thanks to all of the players in Renaissance for creating music that I have enjoyed for over 46 years now, ever since I first heard *Turn Of The Cards* playing in a record store in Topeka, Kansas in 1974.

Thanks, finally, to everyone who chooses to read this. I hope you enjoy it!

Would you like to write for Sonicbond Publishing?

We are mainly a music publisher, but we also occasionally publish in other genres including film and television. At Sonicbond Publishing we are always on the look-out for authors, particularly for our two main series, On Track and Decades.

Mixing fact with in depth analysis, the On Track series examines the entire recorded work of a particular musical artist or group. All genres are considered from easy listening and jazz to 60s soul to 90s pop, via rock and metal.

The Decades series singles out a particular decade in an artist or group's history and focuses on that decade in more detail than may be allowed in the On Track series.

While professional writing experience would, of course, be an advantage, the most important qualification is to have real enthusiasm and knowledge of your subject. First-time authors are welcomed, but the ability to write well in English is essential.

Sonicbond Publishing has distribution throughout Europe and North America, and all our books are also published in E-book form. Authors will be paid a royalty based on sales of their book. Further details about our books are available from www.sonicbondpublishing.com. To contact us, complete the contact form there or email info@sonicbondpublishing.co.uk

on track ...

Renaissance

Contents

Introduction 6
Renaissance (1969) 7
Illusion (1971) 15
Prologue (1972) 26
Ashes Are Burning (1973) 36
Turn Of The Cards (1974) 49
Scheherazade And Other Stories (1975) 62
Novella (1977) 72
A Song For All Seasons (1978) 84
Azure D'Or (1979) 94
Camera Camera (1981) 101
Time-Line (1983) 110
Tuscany (2000) 118
Grandine il Vento (2013)/Symphony Of Light (2014) 123
Live Recordings – Audio And Video 130
Compilation Albums 139
Solo Albums And Other Related Recordings 141

Introduction

Renaissance, the much-beloved but highly underrated English progressive rock band, began life in 1969 as an offshoot of the Yardbirds. Keith Relf and Jim McCarty, who had recently left that iconic blues-rock group, decided to put together a new band that would differ from its predecessor by being more influenced by classical and folk music. Toward that end, they released two albums, in 1969 and 1971. The band then quickly underwent a 100 per cent turnover in personnel, resulting in an entirely new Renaissance – and it is this second incarnation that has achieved the greater impact and recognition. Distinguished by the astonishingly beautiful voice of its lead singer, Annie Haslam, its lengthy, multi-movement, classically inspired compositions, and its unusual-for-rock instrumentation (lots of piano, frequent use of strings, and gently strummed acoustic, rather than electric, guitars), Renaissance released six classic studio albums, and one live double album, between 1972 and 1978. In the late 1970s and early 1980s, the band attempted, with limited success, to move in the direction of the prevailing trends in popular music. However, in the 21st century, amid several changes in personnel, but with Haslam continuing as the band's distinctive voice, Renaissance has returned to its orchestral/symphonic rock roots with two studio albums of new material and multiple live releases featuring contemporary treatments of its 1970s classics. As of today, the band continues to tour, bringing its unique music to new audiences.

Renaissance (1969)

Personnel:
Louis Cennamo: bass
John Hawken: piano, harpsichord
Jim McCarty: drums, percussion, vocals
Jane Relf: vocals, percussion
Keith Relf: vocals, guitar, harmonica
Producer: Paul Samwell-Smith
Release date: late 1969
Highest chart position: 60 (UK)
Running time of original LP: 39:21
Note: This album has been released on CD many times, sometimes with bonus tracks. In one case it was released under the title *Innocence*.

Keith Relf had been the lead singer and harmonica player for The Yardbirds, the legendary English blues and psychedelic rock band that would be inducted into the Rock and Roll Hall of Fame in 1992. He was also an accomplished songwriter, having co-written several of the band's songs, including such top-ten singles as 'Shapes of Things' and 'Over Under Sideways Down'. However, toward the end of his time with the band, his songwriting began to move in a new direction, more in the style of contemporary acoustic folk music. The Yardbirds drummer, Jim McCarty, shared Relf's interest in exploring that style, so in early 1968, following the break-up of the band, they joined forces in forming Together, an acoustic-based duo. But after recording and releasing a single under that name, they quickly realised that in order to take their new act on the road they would need additional players. Thus the idea for a new band, which would come to be called 'Renaissance', was born.

Relf and McCarty agreed that they wanted their new band to take a quieter, more restrained, approach than had been the case with the Yardbirds. They would try to create new folk-inflected music that reflected their admiration for the work of thoughtful contemporary singer-songwriters, like Tim Hardin or Joni Mitchell, but to be presented in a band context, somewhat in the manner of such groups as Fairport Convention and The Incredible String Band.

On the advice of another ex-Yardbird, Chris Dreja, Relf and McCarty invited pianist John Hawken, formerly of the Nashville Teens (a British group, best known for their 1964 top-ten single, 'Tobacco Road'), to audition for a slot in their new band. His playing was impressive, as was that of another player they invited to audition, Louis Cennamo, former bassist for the Herd (a group primarily known for having been fronted by a young Peter Frampton). Hawken's aggressive playing brought another element prominently into the new band's mix – a classical music influence. Indeed, his enthusiasm for classical music was such that he frequently inserted brief quotations from classical pieces into his solos. To the surprise of Relf and McCarty, they found that this worked, and that, as a result, their fledgeling band seemed to be on a path toward creating something new – a melding of rock, folk, and classical – that was unlike anything the world had previously heard.

Only one element was missing. Relf and McCarty had once played a gig in the US in which they shared the bill with the Stone Poneys, a band that featured a young Linda Ronstadt on lead vocals. Inspired by her singing, they thought that a female singer would fit in well with the style they were trying to develop. They decided to give Jane Relf, Keith's sister, a chance, even though she had never sung professionally before. She was eager for the opportunity, and had a pretty, albeit untrained, voice.

Once the line-up was finalised, and they had a few rehearsals under their belt, the band hit the road and played several live gigs before entering the studio to record their first album. Produced by another former Yardbird, bassist Paul Samwell-Smith, this first effort received many negative reviews upon its release but is much more highly regarded today. While the album is certainly open to legitimate, fair-minded, well-informed criticism, some of the criticism it took upon release was undoubtedly based simply on a failure to comprehend what the band was doing – for this hybridisation of genres, developed in songs of unusual length, represented something radically new in the British rock scene. And what is genuinely new tends, at first, to be seen as a failed attempt to do something already established.

But now that we have had ample time in which to familiarise ourselves with what has come to be called 'progressive rock', it is possible to appreciate this first Renaissance album as a pioneering representative of that genre. Indeed, Mike Barnes, in his book, *A New Day Yesterday: UK Progressive Rock and the 1970s*, includes it in his list of just fourteen albums that have a claim on the title of being the first progressive rock album. While he ends up awarding the crown to King Crimson's *In the Court of the Crimson King*, released in October 1969, it is noteworthy that the first Renaissance album was released at about the same time.

'Kings And Queens' 10:55 (Keith Relf/McCarty)

The album opener impresses on many levels. There is nothing tentative about it – no sense that the band is feeling its way toward a new style. Instead, the classical, rock, and jazz elements are brought together to form a coherent and satisfying synthesis. The several distinct sections that comprise this lengthy piece also flow together well.

The most distinctive part of the song begins at about two minutes in. McCarty lays down a rhythm pattern, in which the first two beats of each measure are accented, while the last two are unaccented. Hawken then reinforces this pattern on piano, playing loud piano chords on the first two beats. After establishing this pattern, he starts to embellish it with a higher, right-hand piano part, as he continues the 'BANG BANG soft soft' pattern with his left. A steady, remarkably propulsive, rhythm generated by drums and piano serves as the foundation for Keith Relf's vocals, which now enter at about 2:32, and continue to support him as he delivers the song's lyrics (in a verse/chorus/verse/chorus pattern).

The other sections of the piece all serve to frame the one just described. Hawken begins the song with a florid, aggressive, classically-inflected piano solo, with Cennamo doubling him on bass. After a brief fast passage, Hawken slows down, and at 0:34 the band comes to a complete stop mid-cadence. Hawken then crashes back in with a loud piano chord. Adding to the startling effect of this chord is that it is not the Bb minor that our ear has been led to expect, but instead a Gb major. This surprise chord also pivots our ear toward the key of the verses.

Shortly after the entrance of Hawken's chord, McCarty's drums come in, to be quickly followed by the other players. The entire band then plays a rather anarchic, jazzy improvisation for a little over a minute. Their busy and fast playing eventually slows down, reduces to just Hawken's piano, and then, like other segments of this piece, almost fades to a stop. This very free, unstructured section thus serves to emphasise, by contrast, the tightly composed rhythmic pattern that supports the singing of the song's verses and chorus.

Following the second verse, Cennamo takes over, playing a slow, descending, arpeggiated bass solo, in a new time signature (3/4). After establishing its melody, he is joined by Hawken and McCarty, who repeat the theme several times, but in increasingly elaborate variations, while also playing increasingly louder and faster. Early in the solo, we also hear Jane Relf quietly vocalising wordlessly in the background. Her tempo increases and her part becomes more prominent, as the solo proceeds. After a short interval all of the players but Cennamo drop out, and we hear him softly and slowly repeating the part he had played at the beginning of the solo.

He then transitions to a new section, in which he quietly, and very slowly, plays a simple, two-note back-and-forth pattern. This has an ominous feel, which is accentuated by the soft, rumbling drum accompaniment. (The notes he plays are separated by three whole tones, and this interval, a tritone, was for centuries called 'the devil's interval'. Listening to it here, one can understand why!) The tension builds as Hawken joins in, doubling Cennamo's bass part on his piano; and it builds further as the volume increases and McCarty adds cymbal crashes to the mix.

After a few iterations of this, the rest of the band drops out, and Hawken, continuing to play loudly, begins a solo. At first, he plays a well-defined, presumably composed, melody, but gradually shifts to a free, improvisatory sound, during which he is joined by bass and drums, which are also freely played. Then, led by Hawken's 'call' and Cennamo's response, the band tightens up again and launches into a new riff, this one in 7/8 time. After a brief episode in which the players explore several variations on this new theme, they once again slow down, and then abandon Hawken, who plays arrhythmically for a few seconds (just long enough to allow the listener to leave the band's excursion into septuple meter behind), before coming almost to a complete stop. And that is McCarty's cue to bring back the 'BANG BANG soft soft' rhythm pattern, marking the imminent return of the first verse, to be followed by another iteration of the chorus.

After the final statement of the chorus, Keith Relf performs a fairly quiet guitar solo on top of the same rhythmic foundation that had supported the verses and choruses. He is shortly accompanied by wordless vocals, both male and female. After a brief interval, the entire band, except for Hawken, abruptly drops out, and the pianist plays a repeating part with a distinctive 3 + 3 + 2 pattern of accents. As this pattern repeats, one by one the other band members enter, Hawken layers another piano part on top, and background vocals also join the mix. McCarty begins to drum more aggressively and wildly as the volume increases, adding to the musical tension. But then the section moves in the opposite direction, as McCarty calms down, the background singers drop out, and the tension gradually diminishes until the band rallies to bring the song to a close with one final dramatic flourish.

This beautifully composed and arranged piece is enhanced by outstanding ensemble playing. The performances of Hawken, McCarty, and Cennamo are especially noteworthy. The lyrics, ostensibly about the doings of royalty, also offer something of interest, as lines like 'Jesters' jokes aren't even funny, poking fun at sorrow/ Lords and Ladies hoard their riches fearful for tomorrow' can be read as a witty commentary on the politics of wealth inequality.

'Innocence' 7:05 (Keith Relf/McCarty)

Another genre-blending, multi-part composition, this one lacks the coherence of its predecessor, as its different sections don't connect with one another quite as convincingly, and the psychedelic 1960s rock sound that pervades most of it clashes with the classical style of Hawken's piano solo in the middle. The main ingredient contributing to that psychedelic feel is the persistent use of a wah-wah pedal, used to modify the output, not of Keith Relf's guitar, as one might expect, but rather Hawken's piano. This makes his sudden switch to a classical piano sound all the more incongruous, although the solo itself, ably accompanied by Cennamo on bass, is the highlight of the track.

While Keith Relf handles the lead vocals, another highlight of the song is his sister's brief supporting vocal in the 'If I could show you' chorus, where she comes in at the end of each line, singing a very high part, quite low in the mix.

Although this track does not sound much like 'Kings and Queens', one can detect some continuity in the movement from the first song to the second, as the two pieces do share some features in common. For example, the '3 + 3 +2' rhythmic pattern employed near the end of 'Kings and Queens' is reprised right at the beginning of 'Innocence', and is brought back again at about five and a half minutes in. The same is true of the unusual harmonic pattern (the tonic chord followed by the chord a half-step higher) that was used for the verses of 'Kings and Queens'. It, too, is reprised here, in the same two places just mentioned.

The message of the lyrics seems to be that adults make trouble for themselves by asking too many questions, in contrast to 'a little child' who 'smiles sweetly/ Cause he hasn't had the time/ To learn to ask the question why'. This puzzles me because, in my experience, small children are generally full of curiosity and wonder, and tend to ask 'why' questions far more frequently than do older people.

'Island' 5:57 (Keith Relf/McCarty)

The first track on the album to spotlight Jane Relf on lead vocals, this one features a relatively simple, straightforward arrangement, without abandoning the practice of melding rock with classical music. It begins with a very brief, gently rippling, piano solo, which quickly gives way to a simple pattern of rhythmic guitar strums, alternating between two chords. Drums and bass then join in support of the guitar pattern (a repeating 3 + 3 + 2 rhythm, identical to that used in portions of the album's first two songs), and this serves as the background against which Jane Relf delivers her vocals, in the form of three verses, with a chorus introduced after the first verse and repeated after each succeeding verse. Beginning with the first statement of the chorus, and continuing through the other verses and iterations of the chorus, two changes occur: she is joined in singing by her brother (who sings exactly the same melody, but an octave lower), and Hawken's piano enters and quickly replaces the guitar as the dominant instrument in support of the vocals. The melody and the singing are both pleasant enough (though Jane Relf's intonation is at times approximate, rather than precisely accurate), as are the rather innocuous lyrics, which simply express a desire to live on an ideal island.

But then the song transitions, rather abruptly and seemingly arbitrarily, to a classical piano solo, supported by bass and cymbals. The piece they play here is not original, however, but rather an uncredited quotation from Beethoven's *Piano Sonata No. 8 in C minor, Op. 13* (commonly known as *Sonata Pathétique*). Hawken plays Beethoven well, and Cennamo's and McCarty's parts, both excellently executed, do add something to what is normally heard as a solo piano piece. The only problem with this section, aside from ethical issues concerning plagiarism, is that its juxtaposition with the musically unrelated first part of the song makes for a rather disjointed track.

Toward the end of the piece Jane Relf adds some lovely wordless vocals, after which, at 5:25, Hawken and Cennamo close it out with a brief, rapidly paced, classical flourish – another quotation from Beethoven's *Sonata Pathétique*, in this case, the opening part of the last movement, 'Rondo'. Throughout this track, and elsewhere, Cennamo shows himself to be quite at home playing classical music, and also adept at playing lightning-fast bass runs cleanly.

'Island' is noteworthy for having been the song Annie Haslam would go on to sing at her successful late 1970 audition for the (then vacant) female vocalist slot. It also has the distinction of being the only pre-Haslam era song to be included on a Haslam era Renaissance album, 2018's *A Symphonic Journey*.

'Wanderer' 4:00 (Hawken/McCarty)

This is the shortest track on the album and the only one for which Hawken receives a writing credit. Structurally, it is the mirror image of 'Island'. Rather than beginning with a section featuring Jane Relf's vocals and then segueing into a keyboard-based instrumental finale, here those elements are presented in reverse order.

This time Hawken's keyboard of choice is the harpsichord, rather than piano, and it both carries the melody in the opening, instrumental, section, and provides the most substantial accompaniment to the vocals in the song's latter half. At first, Hawken plays it in a baroque style more reminiscent of Bach or Vivaldi than Beethoven. But during the vocal section, his style changes and he confines himself mostly to arpeggiated chords as if he were a fingerpicking guitarist accompanying a folk singer. A folk flavour is also imparted by the absence of drums during the vocal parts, with percussion being limited to tambourine. The minor key vocal melody of this song, while rather simple, is affecting, despite receiving little help in this regard from the rather vague lyrics. And the song improves on its two immediate predecessors in that its two main sections sound as though they both belong together in the same piece.

'Bullet' 11:24 (Keith Relf/McCarty)

This is the longest, loosest, jazziest, and most psychedelic track on the album. The overall structure is sufficiently free as to allow any of its individual sections to be developed further, without limit, through improvisation – which can come in handy when there is a need to fill up one's time slot during a live gig.

The piece opens with a simple, rhythmic, rumbling drum part, which starts quietly, and then slowly and steadily becomes louder. Hawken shortly joins in with a minor-key melody on piano, which is eventually punctuated with cymbal crashes. A brief bass and piano duet then closes out this opening instrumental section and serves as a transition to the song's only vocal section with lyrics.

Here the entire band (bass, drums, piano, and guitar) quietly lays down a steady 4/4 rock groove, on top of which multiple voices then begin to sing, also somewhat quietly, something like 'Hey Lady Sodom Ramanah', over and over again in unison. Shortly thereafter Keith Relf begins to sing a rather tuneless lead vocal, with the 'Hey Lady Sodom Ramanah' chant continuing in the background. As this happens the volume and intensity of the instrumental backing, especially McCarty's drumming, gradually increases, as does the distortion applied to Relf's voice, so that, by the third verse, he sounds deranged – an effect that the bizarre lyrics only serve to enhance. (Consider the first verse: 'Black mamba bamboo business/ on a red sun night/ All over cry forgiveness/ for the last gunfight'. Confused? Maybe the next verse will clear it up for you: 'So cool in your compensation/ that you keep next to your skin/ Cold sudden shock reminder/ that you can't come in'.)

This section is brought to an abrupt end by Hawken's insertion of a dissonant piano chord, which he then repeats several times, accompanied by McCarty's free, energetic drumming. (Though in a different key, this is otherwise the same chord that is featured near the end of Gustav Holst's 'Mars, the Bringer of War', from his famous orchestral suite, *The Planets*.) When this dies out Hawken establishes a new, steady, rhythmic background pattern, over which Keith Relf begins a highly distorted harmonica solo. As he proceeds the rest of the band joins in, and as their playing quickly intensifies, they create a very effective, highly energised, rock groove, in spite of the fact that their riffing takes place within the context of a single, unchanging, chord (E major).

At the conclusion of Relf's solo the band, while maintaining its groove, shifts to a new chord, then to another, then to a reiteration of that two-chord sequence. Hawken then abruptly changes the mood, as he reintroduces the dissonant Holst chord, striking it eight times while McCarty drums furiously in the background. The tempo and volume both slacken during the last two or three iterations of this chord. After coming almost to a complete stop, the drums come back in before Hawken re-enters to play the chord again, repeatedly, but this time in a distinctive 5/4 rhythm pattern that makes it clear that he is directly quoting (though, once again, without attribution) from Holst's masterpiece.

The 'Mars' quotation is followed by some loose, unstructured noodling on bass, drums, and piano, after which the band comes to a dead stop. After two seconds of silence, Cennamo takes over with a bass cadenza. He plays unaccompanied for well over two minutes, ending, perhaps in a call back to 'Kings and Queens', on a tritone.

He is then joined by wordless, choir-like vocals. Cennamo's bass fades out rather quickly as these voices gain volume. As they have been skilfully recorded, perhaps in an environment well suited to bringing out their synchronous resonance, the effect is otherworldly and bears a close resemblance to the sound Stanley Kubrick used in the famous 'monolith' scenes in his classic 1968 film *2001: A Space Odyssey*. As the voices persist, they continuously undergo subtle modulations. Since the singing is quite high in spots, the principal vocalist is presumably Jane Relf. We next begin to hear some gently played bells or chimes, as well as wind effects. The wind sounds gradually increase in volume as the other sounds progressively decrease before the track begins its fade to silence.

This epic track, which closes out the original LP, is by far the most controversial one on the album. Some exalt its eclectic variety, its experimental feel, its trippiness, and the virtuosity of Cennamo's unaccompanied bass solo and of Samwell-Smith's production in the final spacey vocal section. Others find it undisciplined, disjointed, unmelodic, lyrically incoherent, and overly long. It would not be the last Renaissance piece to provoke such divergent reactions.

Related Tracks
'Shining Where The Sun Has Been' 2:52 (McCarty/Keith Relf)
Following the demise of the Yardbirds, McCarty and Keith Relf initially formed a short-lived acoustic duo, called 'Together', before moving on to found Renaissance. This duo recording, however, was made in the summer of 1968, before the Yardbirds had disbanded. It is a simple tune, about a simple subject (being in love while delighting in the joys of summer), set to a simple arrangement, just two voices and two acoustic guitars. The sound quality is very rough – a further indication that this is probably a demo, not intended for release, rather than a polished, professionally produced recording.

It is available as a bonus track on the Mooncrest label CD release of the debut album, here misleadingly titled *Innocence*, as well as on *Innocents & Illusions*, a double CD set containing both *Renaissance* and *Illusion* (Renaissance's second album), in addition to bonus tracks.

'The Sea' 3:05 (Keith Relf/McCarty)

This B-side to a January 1970 single release, featuring a Jane Relf lead vocal, is included as a bonus track on multiple CD versions of the album. Lyrically this short song resembles 'Island', in that it, too, is about a desire to live in an exotic, faraway location. It is noteworthy that this piece includes an extended passage in which Relf sings a portion of the melody wordlessly, in a manner that will become increasingly associated with Renaissance's style following Annie Haslam's ascension to the lead vocalist position.

The A-side to this single, a shortened version of 'Island', in which the track fades out prior to the start of Hawken's piano solo, is also included on CDs that contain 'The Sea'.

'No Name Raga' 14:23 (Keith Relf/McCarty)

Recorded live at the Fillmore West in San Francisco on 6 March 1970, this is a piece that has never been released (and probably never recorded) in a studio version.

Ragas are central to the classical music traditions of India. To my ears, this freewheeling psychedelic jam does not sound Indian, though several of its sections do convey a vaguely eastern feel. This performance features freaky vocals by both Relf siblings, a fair amount of wah-wah piano from Hawken, and far more electric guitar soloing from Keith Relf than would ever make its way onto a Renaissance studio recording.

The sound quality is far from ideal, but not bad for a 1970 live performance that was probably not professionally recorded. In any case, it is certainly listenable.

It is available on the CD *Live Fillmore West 1970* (also known as *Live + Direct*), as well as the CD *Past Orbits of Dust*, which, with the exception of one studio outtake, is a collection of live recordings from several different venues. (The recording of 'No Name Raga' is the same Fillmore West version as appears on the other album.)

Illusion (1971)

Personnel:
Louis Cennamo: bass
John Hawken: piano, keyboards
Jim McCarty: drums, vocals
Jane Relf: vocals, percussion
Keith Relf: guitar, vocals
Terry Crowe: lead vocals on 'Mr. Pine'
Michael Dunford: guitar on 'Mr. Pine'
Neil Korner: bass on 'Mr. Pine'
Terry Slade: drums on 'Mr. Pine'
Don Shinn: electric piano on 'Past Orbits of Dust'
Producer: Keith Relf
Release date: early 1971
Highest chart position: Did not chart
Running time of original LP: 42:31

The original incarnation of Renaissance fell apart during the recording of
Illusion, the band's second album. Prominent among the reasons for this
dissolution was the band members' dissatisfaction with their experiences
on the road. Following the release of its first album, Renaissance had toured
America, mostly as a support act, since it was a new, relatively unknown, group,
and therefore had not established enough fan interest to be able to sell many
tickets as a headliner. This caused multiple problems:

To begin with, American audiences can be very rude to warm-up acts, and,
at best, tend not to give them an attentive and sympathetic hearing. But to
the extent that some concertgoers were curious to hear the new band, it was
generally because they knew that two members of the legendary Yardbirds
were in it. Thus, they wanted to hear Yardbirds hits, and perhaps other tunes
that would at least be in a similar style. Playing against such expectations, it
was almost inevitable that the new band would disappoint. To illustrate this
point, recall that the single thing for which the Yardbirds were most known
was the guitar heroics of Eric Clapton, Jeff Beck, and Jimmy Page, the three
legendary figures who had taken turns serving as that band's lead guitarist.
Renaissance, in quite radical contrast, was specifically intended not to be a
guitar-based band, and its relatively unspectacular and undemanding guitar
parts were handled by Keith Relf, who had mostly stuck to singing and playing
the harmonica in the Yardbirds. It is thus not surprising to read in McCarty's
autobiography, *Nobody Told Me!*, of an incident in which McCarty tried to take
a glance at Relf while he was playing a guitar solo, only to spot him 'hiding
behind the grand piano, out of sight of the entire audience'.

Additionally, McCarty and Relf, who were already somewhat tired of the
rigours of touring as a headliner, found that touring as a support act was vastly
worse, 'because everything from accommodation and transport, to the state of
the dressing room and the way promoters treat you is designed to make the
headliners feel good...or, at least, less wretched than the support act'.

Things came to a head during the recording of *Illusion*. Studio dates were booked before the band was ready – they had prepared only two songs. Also, while they had used an independent producer, ex-Yardbird Paul Samwell-Smith, for their first album, this time a band member, Keith Relf, decided that he should produce, and this, at least in McCarty's telling, also caused problems. According to McCarty, when John Hawken stumbled a bit on the band's first run-through of 'Past Orbits of Dust', a long, jazzy number, Relf did not do the expected thing, which would have been to offer a few words of encouragement before simply letting him try again. Instead, he immediately took the more radical step of bringing in an outside player, Don Schinn, who had more experience playing jazz. McCarty comments: 'We all know the kind of resentments that can bring. Tempers were fraying; petty rows were breaking out ... Situations escalated for no reason, imagined slights became international incidents ... With the second album still incomplete, I announced I was leaving and was stunned when first Keith, then Louis, said that they'd had enough, too'.

In addition to the bad feelings generated by these interpersonal squabbles, it seems that the two ex-Yardbirds had by this point simply grown weary of the endless touring/recording/touring again/recording again treadmill attendant to being a member of a working rock band. Both of them wanted (and in the case of Keith Relf, this was partly because of health issues) to take a break from performing, and to concentrate, instead, on writing. McCarty's plan, initially, was not to break with the band completely, but rather to continue his involvement behind the scenes, primarily through his songwriting. And indeed, the Haslam era Renaissance would go on to record four of his compositions.

But the abrupt resignation of McCarty, Cennamo, and Keith Relf as performing band members left Hawken and Jane Relf with a serious problem, as the album was at that point unfinished. While several tracks had been completed, these alone would have resulted in an unacceptably short album. At least one more track would be needed. So Hawken brought in drummer Terry Slade, as well as the remainder of his former Nashville Teens bandmates – guitarist Michael Dunford, bassist Neil Korner, and singer Terry Crowe – and they played on a Dunford composition, 'Mr. Pine', to complete the album.

Given the troubled circumstances of its production, and the fact that most of its principal players had now left the band, it is unsurprising that no record company was willing to invest in promoting this album, and few were interested in releasing it. Thus, its initial release, in 1971, was limited to Germany. It began to be released elsewhere in 1973, as by then the growing popularity of the Haslam-fronted band had sparked interest in the band's back catalogue. It would not be released in the UK until 1977.

Of historical significance is the fact that the two songwriters who would eventually team up to write almost all of the most famous and highly regarded songs in the Renaissance catalogue, composer Michael Dunford and lyricist Betty Thatcher, both received their first Renaissance writing credits on this album, though here they were writing separately, rather than collaborating. Thatcher, a poet, was a friend of Jane Relf, who put her in touch with McCarty, with the idea that he might be able to set her lyrics to music. They collaborated by mail, resulting, on this album, in two songs.

'Love Goes On' 2:51 (Keith Relf)

The shortest, poppiest, and most repetitive Renaissance track to this point, 'Love Goes On' sounds like a failed attempt at a hit single. Very little of the musical complexity of the first album is in evidence here, and there are no extended instrumental passages. The lyrical content is almost unbearably slight, consisting, aside from one short verse in the middle, of 23 explicit statements of the fact that 'love goes on'.

But the track is not without its merits. In the middle there is a brief break from the relentless 'love goes on' part, during which Jane Relf sings the song's one verse, and one immediately notices that she sounds much better than she did on the first album, bringing a sweeter tone, along with greater power and conviction than was apparent in any of her earlier vocal performances. As the melody of this verse is also quite agreeable, the piece might have been improved by repeating it a couple of times by adding verses, while cutting a few of the reminders that 'love goes on'.

Moreover, the monotony of the repetition in the 'love goes on' sections is somewhat relieved by the moderate complexity of their three-part vocal arrangement. The first part starts just one second into the song. As it continues, a second part enters, followed shortly by Jane Relf's high harmony, at which point the interweaving of the three vocal lines creates a pleasing effect.

Finally, to note a significant change from the first album, the very first sound we hear in this track is Keith Relf's acoustic guitar, and his gentle, folk-inflected strumming is featured prominently throughout most of the song (the exception being the Jane Relf solo verse in the middle). On the first album, by contrast, guitar was used sparingly (as Hawken's piano dominated), and, when it was used, it tended to be an electric guitar – surprisingly so, given that McCarty and Keith Relf were writing the band's songs on acoustic guitars, and had announced that they intended to take the band in a quiet, folkish direction.

'Golden Thread' 8:15 (McCarty/Keith Relf)

When the band's pre-booked studio time arrived, they had only two songs that were fully worked out and ready to record. This was one of them, and it shows. Featuring a lengthy, well-constructed, multi-section form, this track revives some of the classical music feel that had been so prevalent on the first album. By far the most impressive aspect of the song is its many passages of multi-voice, choir-like, wordless vocalising, both in support of McCarty's lead vocal and, more frequently, on their own, as the main conveyor of melody.

Hawken's piano leads the way in the piece's opening, instrumental, passage, as he plays, frequently accompanied by Cennamo's bass and Keith Relf's electric guitar, in a classical music style. When McCarty's drums come in, the band shifts to a steady, rhythmic, rock-style 4/4 beat. At the two-minute mark, Jane Relf enters, singing a lovely wordless melody. The band then changes suddenly, yet smoothly, to a 3/4 time signature, as male voices join in, the melody changes and the wordless vocalising gradually increases in volume. Shortly thereafter there is another smooth transition, this time back to 4/4 time, and to a new, even prettier, melody (henceforth to be called 'melody 2'), carried, once again, by wordless vocals, over a D minor/A minor/C minor/G chord progression. This is a case of a successful melding of genres, as the choir-like singing gives a classical music feel to a chord progression that might otherwise be played as an accompaniment to a folk song.

An expressive aspect of this lovely melody derives from the suspensions – the held melody note from the previous chord – on the A minor and G chords. The suspensions sound perfectly consonant on one chord but give a little frisson of dissonance on the next chord before quickly resolving.

At just after three minutes, the voices stop, and the band begins to create another steady, rhythmic, rock groove in 4/4, that is nonetheless quite different from the one we had heard initially. Moreover, the playing is rooted in a D major chord, indicating a shift from the tonality of the preceding passage.

This lasts for all of thirteen seconds before the band quietens down to make room for the return of the wordless vocals. They are used to help re-establish the D minor/A minor/C minor/G chord progression, though the singers do not this time sing a melody on top of it, as they had done previously. Instead, they provide the foundation for the first appearance of sung lyrics, as McCarty takes the lead vocal. While his voice is thin, he has no trouble conveying the melody, and his lack of power suggests fragility and vulnerability, which is fitting, given the song's lyrical content. At one point McCarty takes a break from singing lyrics and takes up, instead, a reiteration of melody 2. When he returns to lyrics in singing the song's final verse, he does so in counterpoint with that melody, which continues on its own for a bit after he has finished.

We then get a quick reprise of the D major instrumental section, which, in turn, gives way to a piano-and-bass baroque-style interlude, at a slower tempo. After 25 seconds the players start slowing down even further, before switching to a new melody in D minor, but built on a different chord progression. Hawken and Cennamo are quickly joined by percussion, and, once again, choir-like wordless vocals, but this time in support of a piano melody, rather than a lead vocal. However, as the vocals gradually gain volume, they eventually start to be heard as sharing the melody with Hawken, and then as carrying the melody. After a bit the singers and the percussionist drop out, leaving Hawken and Cennamo to play a short variation on the melody, only to slow down, before nearly coming to a complete stop.

A second or two later, the band comes back in, clearly led by the vocalists, as melody 2 is re-stated, this time hummed, rather than sung on the full-throated 'aah' syllable as before. From a quiet beginning, the passage quickly gets louder and louder, before, just as quickly, starting its fade to the silence that ends the piece.

Aside from the pretty minor-key melodies that pervade the song, and the beautiful sound of its wordless vocals, the most impressive aspect of this track is that its many rapid transitions from one section to another always sound smooth and natural. Nothing sounds jarring or disjointed. So what we have here is a lengthy, experimental, multi-section piece that successfully blends baroque, classical, folk, and rock styles – in short, a fine specimen of progressive rock.

'Love Is All' 3:40 (McCarty/Thatcher)

Like 'Love Goes On', this is a short, highly repetitive, pop song, lacking in the variety and complexity of the more ambitious Renaissance pieces. It is built on a very simple four-chord progression (F/C/G/A minor), which runs throughout the song, encompassing the instrumental introduction, the verses, and the chorus.

This is the first of two songs on the album to feature lyrics by Betty Thatcher, who would go on to become the band's principal lyricist. This is one of her weakest efforts, as it consists of nothing but statements about love that are either banal ('everywhere love is love'), or else so vague as to be virtually meaningless (the endlessly repeated chorus, 'Love is all, love is one, love is one').

On the positive side, there's no denying that the tune is catchy and that Hawken's piano is lovely, both during his baroque-inflected introduction and as he accompanies the singing.

Like the first two tracks on this album, but unlike anything on the band's debut, this one places almost all of its emphasis on vocals, and includes no extended instrumental sections. Keith Relf takes the lead vocal, and at first, conveys the song's infectious melody by himself. But when his sister and McCarty join him in the chorus, and all three vocalists sing joyously in unison, the track begins to sparkle. Then, in the second verse, the band returns to its technique of supporting the lead vocal with wordless vocal harmonising, adding warmth, and a fullness of sound, which had been lacking during the solo reading of the first verse.

The instrumental backing intensifies gradually as the song unfolds, with Keith Relf adding some tasteful fuzz-tone lead guitar licks in the background when the chorus comes around again after the second verse. After one final verse (featuring wordless harmonising again), he resumes his restrained, but slightly psychedelic, playing, this time sustaining it through the many repetitions of the maddeningly catchy chorus before the track finally fades to silence.

'Mr. Pine' 7:00 (Dunford)

This is the track that was recorded after McCarty, Cennamo, and Keith Relf had quit the band in the midst of the *Illusion* sessions, necessitating the immediate hiring of replacements. The most important of these was Michael Dunford, who would eventually become the band's principal composer and guitarist. This song is significant in that it is the first of his compositions to be recorded by Renaissance.

Hawken's harpsichord starts it off, shortly to be joined by the quiet, tuneful lead vocal of new recruit, Terry Crowe. He sings two verses, and on the first line of each, he is joined by Jane Relf. Their voices compliment each other well, and she is missed when she drops out, leaving Crowe to fend for himself, on lines two and three. He then speaks, rather than sings, the last line of each verse, the final word of which is drenched in echo, furthering the kaleidoscopic vibe that the arrangement had already established. At the conclusion of the second verse, the harpsichord-led backing continues for a bit, after which the track begins to fade before coming to a complete stop.

When it starts up again, about four seconds later, Hawken has moved on from harpsichord to organ. After a brief introduction, he applies a wah-wah pedal to it and plays a melody that is compelling enough on its own, but that bears little musical resemblance to the song's first section. It is a melody that composer Dunford will later recycle and insert into the epic 'Running Hard' on Renaissance's 1974 album, *Turn of the Cards*. At 3:20 Crowe and Relf join forces for an ascending, wordless, choir-like vocal line – another part that will ultimately make its way into 'Running Hard'.

This gives way to some aggressive acoustic guitar strumming from Dunford, which serves as the foundation for a rocking Hawken organ solo, followed by two lyrical stanzas, each with a new vocal melody – one, mixed down low and possibly sung by Relf, and the other, much higher in the mix, taken by Crowe. These are followed by Dunford's brief, acid-drenched, electric guitar solo.

About twenty seconds later the track starts to fade out and is ultimately reduced almost to silence, before fading back in with a reprise of the song's opening structure: a Hawken harpsichord line, followed by the singing of a final verse. Here we find the same vocal arrangement as was used for the first two verses, except that this time the trippy echo effect is applied to the entirety of the final, spoken, line, rather than just to the last word. The song then concludes with a wordless 'la-la-la' vocal part from both singers, backed by harpsichord – a section that lasts less than 30 seconds before the track fades to its final silence.

One of Dunford's principal strengths as a songwriter, his talent for melody, is already strongly in evidence in this early composition, as every bit of it is musically interesting, and one's attention never flags over the course of its seven minutes.

Two weaknesses are also apparent, but they are ones that he would soon overcome. The first weakness is a failure to integrate the different musical sections of this piece so as to make them into a unified whole, rather than a disconnected series of fragments. One surmises that he worked to correct this, as most of his subsequent lengthy, multi-section compositions flow together well, with the different sections complementing each other to an unusually high degree.

The second failing is in the area of lyrics, as the words to 'Mr. Pine' indicate a willingness to juxtapose lines on the basis of rhyme alone, with no consideration of any other poetic value. Don't believe me? Here's the first verse: 'Oh, Mr. Pine/ Doesn't wait till after nine/ There's not a friend he's had to buy/ Keeps his head above the sky/Ain't got much, and he don't ask why'. The whole song is like that.

Dunford's solution to this problem was straightforward and completely effective – he gave up lyric writing, choosing instead to concentrate on composing, and to leave the lyrics to a collaborator, who would turn out to be Betty Thatcher.

'Face Of Yesterday' 6:06 (McCarty)

When the *Illusion* recording sessions began, this was the only song, aside from 'Golden Thread', that the band brought to the sessions as a fully worked out composition, ready to record.

Hawken's piano starts it off with a short chord sequence suggestive of church music. He quickly transitions to a lively classical style melody, accompanied by Cennamo's contrapuntal bass lines. (Cennamo's very active bass playing, placed high in the mix, is noticeable throughout the track.)

At about 35 seconds in, Keith Relf's acoustic guitar enters and establishes the harmonic pattern that will dominate the song, a simple alteration of two major seventh chords, played in the same '3 + 3 +2' rhythmic pattern that can be heard in three other songs that McCarty had a hand in composing: 'Kings and Queens', 'Innocence', and 'Island'. The ambiguity inherent in major seventh chords is exploited skilfully here. On the one hand, they sound light, open, and spacious, and thus generate a warm feeling. But they also contain just enough dissonance to introduce an element of wistfulness or melancholy, and that is the feeling that Jane Relf, here in her best, most natural range, conveys when she places her vocal on top of the major seventh chords.

Each of the three verses she sings tells of an individual (in order, a sculptor, a builder, and a composer) who experienced disappointment when his creation did not come out well, with the result that it was soon forgotten – becoming a 'face of yesterday'.

A somewhat surprising element in the instrumental accompaniment to her singing is the inclusion of some intermittent electric guitar lead lines from her brother. These unobtrusive lines are kept low in the mix, but they blend in well with the piano, bass, and drum parts, as well as with Keith Relf's own acoustic guitar strumming.

At the completion of the second verse, the major seventh harmonic pattern is temporarily dropped, and we hear Jane Relf sing a new melody (superior, in my judgment, to that of the verses), in a wordless, 'ba-ba-da', style, with the opening piano melody also mingled into this passage a couple of times.

When the major seventh chords return, along with the '3 + 3 +2' rhythmic pattern, at first they are joined by some wordless 'ah, ah' singing in the background, before giving way to Relf's rendition of the third verse.

At its conclusion, we get a reiteration of the 'ba-ba-da' chorus, which eventually turns into a two-part stretto, as a male voice (probably that of brother Keith), takes up the same chorus, but with their two parts, based on and sung over the opening piano and bass duet, interweaving harmoniously by means of deliberate non-alignment.

This gives way to the same churchy piano part that kicked off the track, before Hawken concludes the piece by striking a C major chord and holding it, letting it, and the entire track, fade to silence – frustrating the listener's desire to hear the sequence resolve to an F major chord. Is this perhaps deliberately intended to disappoint us, so that we will share in the disappointment that the subjects of the song felt when they were confronted with the imperfections of their work?

It is noteworthy that when McCarty, Cennamo, Hawken, and Jane Relf reunited to form a new band, called Illusion, they included a new recording of this song on their first album, *Out of the Mist*.

'Past Orbits Of Dust' 14:39 (McCarty/Keith Relf/Thatcher)

The album closer, this is the longest track on either of the first two albums. Despite what one might expect, given its length, this one is not a multi-movement suite, but rather an extended jazzy jam. Because of its many improvisational instrumental breaks, this piece, even more so than 'Bullet', its counterpart on the debut album, readily lends itself to indefinite extension in live performance.

This is the track on which Keith Relf, in his capacity as the album's producer, took the keyboard part away from Hawken and assigned it to a guest musician, Don Shinn. In McCarty's autobiography, he tells us that Relf was unpredictable, and 'could swing, as John Hawken discovered in the studio that time, from being your best mate and solid cheerleader to telling you that you weren't good enough to play the piano on a song you'd helped to arrange in the first place'. On McCarty's version of events, this was one of the moments that led to the dissolution of the original Renaissance line-up.

In any case, the substitution of Shinn for Hawken perhaps explains the jazz-rock feel of the track, and its absence of a classical music element, as Hawken was the band's player most at home with classical music, whereas Shinn was more oriented toward jazz.

In the midst of the jazz-inflected instrumental breaks, there are intermittent vocal sections, in which the Relf siblings sing Betty Thatcher's lyrics. Though more suggestive than literal, these lyrics are clearly about the scientific discovery that human beings are mostly made of stardust (hence the title – we are 'past orbits of dust'). In terms of quality, they represent an improvement by several orders of magnitude over the standard set by her work in 'Love is All', her other contribution to this album.

The piece begins as a jazzy instrumental, as McCarty's drums and Cennamo's bass are quickly joined by Shinn's electric piano, which takes the lead. About twenty seconds in, the players start to establish a steady, highly rhythmic, rock groove, over which the Relfs shortly begin to sing the song's first two verses, mostly in unison.

Just after the conclusion of the first round of singing, the band switches to 6/8 time, on top of which Jane Relf shortly comes back to sing the next section alone. The vocal melody here, which she delivers in her lower register, is different from the one she had previously sung with her brother.

Following her singing of four lyrical lines, the band, continuing in 6/8, enters another jazz jam phase, with Shinn, mixed high (as he is throughout), once again taking the lead. About a minute later, Jane comes back to sing the remaining four lines of this middle vocal section, before yielding back to the jam.

During this long instrumental section, the band attempts, at several points, to break up the monotony by changing some of the elements, or by adding new ones. First, Keith Relf comes in with some note clusters on electric guitar in which the order of the attack and the decay is reversed, suggesting that this part may have been recorded backwards. Next, hand drums (perhaps congas or bongos) are introduced. While these are played quietly, and haltingly, at first, they become progressively more prominent in the mix until Shinn's electric piano takes a break, at which time the hand drums perform a solo, supported just by light drum kit playing (mostly cymbals).

When the hand drums drop out, McCarty takes charge, quickly followed by Cennamo's bass, and then Shinn's electric piano, as the band shifts from its 6/8 time signature back to the driving, 4/4, rock beat it had used to back the first vocal section. And this signals the return of the Relf siblings to sing the song's remaining lyrics, set to the melody of the original vocal section.

At about ten minutes in the vocals conclude for the final time, as the band returns to a 6/8 time signature, and Shinn takes an extended solo over the band's jazzy background. After 90 seconds of this the band starts to slow down, get quieter, and transition to the track's final section – a three-minute episode of free, arrhythmic noodling, which, in the end, gradually, and very quietly, arrives at its final silence.

Like 'Bullet', this is a 'parting of the ways' track, as listeners tend either to regard it as one of the best early Renaissance tracks, or (in significantly greater numbers) one of the worst, with very few placing it anywhere near the middle. One suspects that this is the piece McCarty had in mind when he commented, with reference to the *Illusion* album, 'We should have included more actual songs and less florid improvisation'.

Related Tracks
'Statues' 2:31 (Keith Relf/McCarty)
This short track, featuring a Jane Relf lead vocal, is an outtake from the *Illusion* sessions. For the most part, it is a fairly generic pop song, one that could have been produced by any one of a thousand bands of the period. But what marks it as a Renaissance piece is the fact that its catchy chorus, clearly the song's hook, is in 7/8, a decidedly non-standard time signature. McCarty, in response to an interviewer's question, has stated that he does not remember why it was not included on the album.

It is available as the only studio track on the otherwise live album *Past Orbits of Dust*, and as one of the studio bonus tracks on *Live Fillmore West 1970* (aka *Live + Direct*).

'Try Believing' 2:48 (Keith Relf/McCarty)
A demo that McCarty and Keith Relf made as a duo in 1970, shortly after leaving Renaissance, this pedestrian tune is matched by equally banal lyrics, as in the repeated refrain, 'Try believing, baby, I'm the one'.

It is one of the studio bonus tracks on *Live Fillmore West 1970* (aka *Live + Direct*).

'Widdicombe Fair' 9:35 (Heath)

Shortly after completing *Illusion*, Hawken and Jane Relf left the band and were replaced by pianist John Tout and vocalist Binky Cullom, who joined the remaining players who had performed on 'Mr. Pine' (Crowe, Dunford, Korner, and Slade) in a short-lived, transitional version of Renaissance. While this configuration of players never issued any audio recordings, they did perform five songs, as Renaissance, on a Belgian television program in 1970. Those performances have been released on a DVD, entitled *Kings & Queens*. One of the five songs, 'Widdicombe Fair', appears on no other Renaissance record. (The rest of the DVD is discussed in the separate chapter on live recordings.)

Lead singer Terry Crowe introduces the song to the audience as 'an old English folk song'. And indeed, it had been published as early as 1891 (in the book *Songs and Ballads of the West*), and recorded as early as 1910 (by Charles Tree, a baritone – it is in his recording that the composer credit, 'Heath', appears). Significantly, The Nashville Teens, the band of which Crowe, Dunford, and Korner were alumni, had also recorded a version – undoubtedly the blueprint for this Renaissance interpretation.

As performed on the DVD, the song is very slight, and not very folky. It merely serves as a framework for an extended rock jam. Dunford, on electric guitar, and Tout, on piano, both solo, with Dunford doing so at some length.

'Prayer For Light' 5:27 (McCarty/Keith Relf)

This is a selection from the soundtrack, produced by Keith Relf, for the 1971 movie *Schizom*. It is somewhat reminiscent of 'Golden Thread', as both tracks feature a McCarty lead vocal, a pretty, minor-key melody, and plenty of wordless backing vocals. An unexpected, but effective, feature of the arrangement is that its ending, lasting a good half-minute, is given over to a McCarty drum solo, played very quietly, mostly by tapping gently on cymbals.

The song is included as a bonus track on *Innocence*, as well as on *Innocents & Illusions*.

'Walking Away' 4:19 (Keith Relf/McCarty)

Like 'Prayer for Light', this is from the *Schizom* soundtrack and is included as a bonus track on *Innocence*, as well as on *Innocents & Illusions*. Once again McCarty takes the lead vocal, singing on top of the same '3 + 3 +2' rhythmic pattern that one finds in several Renaissance songs, here established on acoustic guitar. The instrumental sections, which take up the majority of the track, are especially outstanding. The pan flute, an instrument not heard on many Renaissance recordings, takes a solo, as does a classical guitar. And following the last verse, which is hummed, rather than sung, the final two minutes and thirteen seconds of the piece are mostly devoted to a pan flute and classical guitar duet.

'I'd Love To Love You Till Tomorrow' 2:53 (Keith Relf)

This is an early 1976 demo that Keith Relf made at home with his sister, Jane.

He was between bands at the time, but still writing songs and making demos in preparation for new musical projects. Sadly, these plans were never realized, as he died in his home in May 1976, at age 33, from a horrific accident in which he was electrocuted while playing an electric guitar.

The quality of the song is difficult to evaluate because of the extremely stripped-down nature of the arrangement in the demo – just unison vocals by the Relf siblings, accompanied by Keith strumming chords on a twelve-string acoustic guitar. Perhaps some harmony vocals and additional accompaniment would have brought out something that is lacking in this version.

This demo is one of the studio bonus tracks on *Live Fillmore West 1970* (aka *Live + Direct*).

'All The Falling Angels' 5:28 (Keith Relf)

This is Keith Relf's last recording, made ten days before his death. It would eventually be released, in 1989, and only in the US, as the B-side of a single.

At this point in his life, things were not going well for him. His physical health was poor, as he suffered from asthma and emphysema. He was separated from his wife, and, as a result, sometimes separated from his young sons. He was struggling professionally, as none of his post-Yardbirds projects had lasted long or been particularly successful. And, largely because of that, he lacked financial security. All of this is perhaps relevant to the appreciation of this recording. Relf's vocal performance on it is unusually passionate and highly affecting, as he sings in his upper register, and sometimes strains to hit notes outside of his vocal range, giving to the song a strong feeling of intensity and urgency. It is a moving experience to hear someone sing with such pathetic desperation, and its poignancy is only intensified by one's knowledge that the singer is a struggling, depressed young person soon to die a sudden, violent death.

This is a full band performance, as Relf, on acoustic twelve-string guitar, is supported by his former Renaissance colleagues, John Hawken on keyboards and Louis Cennamo on bass, in addition to a session drummer.

The song is included as a bonus track on *Innocence*, as well as on *Innocents & Illusions*.

'Please Be Home' 3:20 (McCarty)

Following Keith Relf's death, the surviving members of the original Renaissance decided to reunite. Since the name 'Renaissance' was unavailable, as the Haslam-fronted band was using it, the players in this new group decided to call themselves 'Illusion', an obvious reference to the second Renaissance album. This track, featuring a Jane Relf lead vocal, is a recording by this new band, although the song ended up not being selected for inclusion on any of Illusion's albums. Though labelled a demo, it sounds like a polished recording, as it is well played and sung, and Relf's singing is ably supported by piano, bass, drums, and a backing vocal, in an arrangement that sounds finished.

This is one of the studio bonus tracks on *Live Fillmore West 1970* (aka *Live + Direct*).

Prologue (1972)

Personnel:
Jon Camp: bass, vocals, tamboura
Annie Haslam: vocals, percussion
Rob Hendry: guitar, mandolin, chimes, backing vocals
Terry Sullivan: drums, percussion
John Tout: piano, organ, string synthesizer, backing vocals
Francis Monkman: VCS3 synthesizer on 'Rajah Khan'
Producer: Miles Copeland and Renaissance
Release date: 1972 (recorded June-July 1972)
Highest chart position: Did not chart
Running time of original LP: 41:17

Following the departures of McCarty, Cennamo, and Keith Relf as performing members, the Renaissance line-up consisted of Hawken, Jane Relf, and new recruits Neil Korner, Michael Dunford, Terry Crowe and Terry Slade – the band that completed the *Illusion* album by recording Dunford's 'Mr. Pine'. This sextet toured Europe in September and October 1970, before it, too, fell apart. Jane Relf quit at the end of the tour and was replaced by an American singer, Annemarie 'Binky' Cullom. During her brief (three month) tenure, Hawken also left, but not before securing his replacement, another pianist with a penchant for classical music, John Tout. While this version of the band (Korner, Dunford, Crowe, Slade, Cullom, and Tout) issued no recordings, it did perform five songs on a Belgian television program, and this performance has been released on a DVD, *Kings and Queens*, released in 2010.

When Cullom decided to move on, Dunford, McCarty (who was still helping out behind the scenes), and Jon Michel, the band's manager, placed an ad, seeking a soprano, in the British weekly music magazine, *Melody Maker*. Annie Haslam, a young, classically trained singer, decided to answer the ad, though her only professional experience to that point had been singing with 'The Gentle People', a group whose regular gig was to perform at a local dinner club. To prepare for the audition, she bought the first Renaissance album, and 'learned it back to front'. The audition was held on New Year's Eve, 1970. In attendance were band members Dunford and Tout, but also McCarty and Keith Relf, who were still to some extent overseeing the band they had started. They asked her to sing 'Island'. The next day she received a phone call informing her that she had won the job. And then, within three weeks, she was in Germany, touring as the newest member of Renaissance.

Because the band already had a lead singer, Terry Crowe, the original idea behind the *Melody Maker* ad was to find a female backing singer who would only occasionally sing lead. And indeed, at first, Haslam was assigned the lead vocal on only one song in the band's set. But that soon changed, and Crowe departed in spring 1971.

The bass position became a revolving door during this period, as the band, which was touring relentlessly, went through four bassists from spring 1971 to early 1972, with Korner giving way, in succession, to Danny McCulloch, Frank

Farrell, and the legendary John Wetton (who would later establish himself as one of the giant figures in the history of progressive rock, based on his work with King Crimson, UK, and Asia, among other bands).

In early 1972, when Miles Copeland took over as the band's manager, his idea was to rebuild the group on a foundation of four elements: Haslam's voice, Tout's piano, Dunford's compositions, and Thatcher's lyrics. The task, then, was to find supporting players who could best complement those elements. New ads were placed in *Melody Maker*. The ad for a bass player specified that a classical approach, and an ability to handle complex arrangements, was essential. More than 80 musicians auditioned for the spot, which ultimately went to Jon Camp. Ginger Dixon was brought in as the new drummer. And with Dunford abandoning his performing role, so as to concentrate on songwriting, Mick Parsons was selected to be the band's new guitarist. Following a brief European tour it was determined that Dixon wasn't quite suitable, and he was replaced by Terry Sullivan. As the time for recording a new Renaissance album was fast approaching, it seemed, at last, that the right line-up was in place.

But then tragedy struck, as young Mick Parsons was killed in a car crash. Haslam recalls him fondly: 'He was lovely. He was a songwriter. He looked fabulous. He had a great personality. His singing voice was just incredible. And his guitar playing was to die for. It was heart-breaking. I mean, we were just beside ourselves'. The band eventually brought in electric guitarist Rob Hendry as Parsons' replacement for the recording of the new album, *Prologue*. When it was released, a note in the credits read, 'This album is dedicated to Mick Parsons'.

While it was not unusual for bands at this time to experience some turnover in personnel, the case of Renaissance, as it entered the studio in June 1972 to record *Prologue*, was unique. The usual pattern, both then and now, was a gradual transformation, in which first one band member, then another, spaced out over a period of years, might leave and be replaced, with other members remaining, so that there would always be substantial continuity in the makeup of the band. But in the case of Renaissance, none of the players about to perform on its third album had played or sung a single note on its first two. This explains why on some of the band's later live albums one of the members will say, 'this is from our first album' when introducing a song from *Prologue* – for while *Prologue* is not the first Renaissance album, it is the first by *this* Renaissance, this entirely new ensemble of players. Note, in this context, that the very title of the album, *Prologue*, suggests to listeners that they are coming in at the very beginning of something, rather than encountering the third instalment in an on-going series.

Equally unusual is the relationship between the musicians who would be playing and singing the material on this album and the songwriters who had written it. Most bands, then and now, perform some combination of pieces that band members themselves have written and 'cover songs' written (and usually first performed) by other artists unconnected to the band. But the songs on *Prologue* fit into neither category. Of the album's six songs, two are by Dunford alone, two are by Dunford and Thatcher, and two are by McCarty and Thatcher. Thus, all of the album's tracks are by songwriters who are affiliated with the band as writers, specifically tasked with providing the band with its material, even though they are not themselves performing members. While it is not unheard of for a band to employ as a lyricist someone who neither sings nor plays on its records (one thinks of Peter Sinfield of King Crimson, or Keith Reid of Procol Harum), I know of no other band that retained, in a nonperforming capacity, a lyricist (Thatcher), a composer (Dunford), and a retired band member who still wanted to stick around and help out a bit, including by composing songs for the band (McCarty).

The involvement of Thatcher, Dunford, and McCarty is also significant in that they, unlike the current performing band members, had contributed to the band's earlier recorded output, with McCarty having written for, and played on, each of the first two albums, Dunford having done the same for a track on *Illusion*, and Thatcher having written lyrics for two songs on that album. This helps to explain some of the similarities between the old and new versions of Renaissance. In both versions, we find: long, multi-section pieces; a strong classical influence, and several classical quotations; the use of piano as the dominant instrument, with guitar de-emphasised; and many female lead vocals. Among the differences, one can note that the original band was somewhat more aggressive, rocked a bit more often, and rocked harder when it did; made greater use of psychedelic effects; made more frequent use of dissonance, odd rhythms, and other kinds of jagged, jarring sounds; and engaged in more jazzy improvisation, including some loose, arrhythmic jamming. The new band, by contrast, was to play songs that were more thoroughly composed, more coherent (in the way that the different sections of the long pieces would flow together and be connected to one another), and much more melodious. The new band would also produce a cleaner, prettier sound, in support of the unusually sweet timbre of the voice of its new lead vocalist.

Prologue is often thought to be the first album in Renaissance's best period, extending from 1972 through 1977. The five studio albums that the band released during this time are extraordinary, containing many excellent tracks, and, to listeners who have a special taste for their style, very few, if any, that are weak, or even mediocre. Having said that, *Prologue* is probably the least successful of these first five albums, as this configuration of the band was new, and the players were still trying to sort out their strengths and weaknesses and figure out just what they wanted to do, and how best to do it. But if this is the weakest of the first five Haslam-era Renaissance albums, that is only because of the surpassing quality of the other four.

'Prologue' 5:35 (Dunford)

Two characteristics of the original Renaissance – the use of piano as the lead instrument, and a heavy reliance on classical music influences – are put on display immediately in this first track by the new Renaissance, as John Tout begins the proceedings with a solo piano performance that quotes Chopin's *Étude Op. 10, No. 12 in C minor* (also known as the *Revolutionary Étude* or the *Étude on the Bombardment of Warsaw*). Just thirteen seconds in the band joins him to establish a steady rock rhythm in the new key of E minor, over which Annie Haslam sings, with Jon Camp providing a backing vocal. Their singing is wordless (they call it 'vocalise', a term that I will henceforth use for wordless vocalising), because Haslam had found, during rehearsals, that she did not like the sound she produced when singing this melody to the words (by Betty Thatcher) that had been intended to serve as the song's lyrics. As she tells it, 'I said, 'Why don't I just sing this?' And it just came out, 'Do do do do do do.'

The melody then takes a turn, and Haslam sings it alone, with no vocal backup, before being joined by Rob Hendry's fuzz-tone electric guitar and Camp's backing vocal, both an octave lower. At first, they perform the same descending melody that she proceeds to sing, only to change, after four notes, to an ascending pattern that harmonises beautifully with her continuing descent.

Following a key change Haslam, as the sole vocalist, sings a six-bar melodic fragment, which she then repeats higher in the scale, and then repeats once more, from an even higher starting point. However, before this last sequence can be concluded, it is replaced by a reprise, played a total of three times, of the earlier descending vocal melody, complete with accompaniment from Hendry's guitar and Camp's voice. This time, however, the melody is in a different key, and Hendry and Camp follow Haslam in her descent, rather than diverging from it in an ascending harmony, as they had previously done. The most important difference, however, is in the rhythm, here an irregular pattern of alternating bars of 3/4 and 4/4 time.

At the conclusion of this episode, Camp comes in with a fast, repeating bass riff, over which Tout plays a brief piano solo. The band then comes to a complete stop, only to start up again almost immediately, in a different key, with a new piano part in a more baroque style, supported by Haslam's quiet background vocalise (this time she sings vowel sounds).

The band then switches key again and drastically slows down the tempo. Haslam proceeds to reprise, at this much slower speed, the vocal melody first heard at the start of the piece. This passage is perhaps the best one in this opening track for appreciating the timbre of Haslam's voice. An interesting touch in this section is Camp's decision to apply a wah-wah peddle to his infrequent, slowly-played, bass notes.

The band, continuing to support Haslam's vocalise solo, then speeds up, thus cueing Haslam and Camp to reprise the song's opening vocal theme, in its original key and at its (just established) original tempo.

Toward the end of the track, the band reprises the earlier section in which Haslam sings a descending melody. But this time as she sings it (with contrasting harmony from Hendry's fuzz-tone guitar and Camp's harmony vocal), the band slows down, and then stops for a fraction of a second, setting the stage for the grand finale – Haslam hitting, and holding, a glorious high note (B5)[1].

'Kiev' 7:36 (McCarty/Thatcher)

Although Betty Thatcher's working relationship with Renaissance had begun through her friendship with Jane Relf, her role as the band's lyricist only increased after the departure of Relf and the other original band members. When Relf introduced her to McCarty, they began to correspond, with Thatcher sending McCarty her lyrics through the mail for him to set to music (this was long before the age of the internet). This sad, minor-key ballad, featuring Thatcher's story of a father grieving alone at the grave of his son, set to McCarty's beautiful Russian-sounding melody, was created in this way.

It begins, as so many Renaissance tracks do, with a rippling classical piano solo. When bass, drums, and guitar join in, they help establish a simple, three-chord pattern, set to a steady 4/4 rhythm, over which Camp begins to sing his lead vocal. He sings about 'a simple man', who led a humble life, with simple pleasures, such as sharing bread with his father. But then the lyrics take a dark turn, as we learn (with Haslam joining in to supply a harmony vocal) that 'the snow fell in Kiev today', and 'the wind drove the mourners away', leaving 'only one man at the grave of Davorian' – and 'this man's heart is too heavy to pray'. At the conclusion of this verse, Haslam, having dropped out for the singing of its last line, comes back in with some vocalise, taking the lead, with Camp now supplying vocal harmony, for some 'nah-nah-nah's.

Camp then returns to lead vocal duties for the second verse. Hendry inserts a new guitar part here, in which the attack and decay of each note is reversed, indicating that they may have been recorded backwards. We learn in this verse that Davorian's father was so grief-stricken at the loss of his son that 'he died there in Kiev today', by the side of his son's grave. This revelation is followed by another round of Haslam-led 'nah-nah-nah' vocalise, toward the end of which the band transitions to a proggy instrumental section, featuring Hendry on mandolin.

Toward the end of this section, the band performs a long, fast, ascending chromatic scale, after which we arrive at yet another classical quotation, as Tout begins to play a passage from Rachmaninoff's famous *Prelude in C-sharp minor*. (The precocious Rachmaninoff wrote it at the age of nineteen, and then suffered the same fate as many other musicians who have had the misfortune of achieving an early monster hit – he could not escape it. During his concert tours, when he would try to perform a program of newer material, audiences would scream, 'C-sharp!', moving him to remark, 'Many, many times I've wished I had never written it'.)

Though Rachmaninoff's melody is different from any of the vocal sections in 'Kiev', the harmonic pattern of 'Kiev' appears to be derived from Rachmaninoff's piece, as the chords underlying both the verses and the 'nah-nah-nah' chorus, though voiced slightly differently, transposed to a different key, and put to a rocking beat, are otherwise almost identical to his. Tout's piano introduction also foreshadows this, as it ends with a similar pattern, paced twice as quickly (in diminution).

When the other players come back in, they rock up Rachmaninoff further, rearranging his piano masterpiece by adding bass, drums, and voices, singing the melody in vocalise. Terry Sullivan's energetic drumming is noteworthy here, as the nature of Renaissance's music often requires him to play quietly, or, for some stretches, to sit out entirely.

At the conclusion of this Rachmaninoff section the band transitions back to one more iteration of the second verse (with a small variation in the last lyrical line), followed by a final occurrence of the 'nah-nah-nah' vocalise, which brings the track to a close, resolving to a major chord on every other phrase, including the final 'nah'.

Camp's vocal performance on this track deserves mention. He would not be assigned many lead vocals during his long tenure with Renaissance, which is understandable given the presence of Haslam in the band's line-up. But here he acquits himself quite well as he brings McCarty's appealing, bittersweet melody to life.

It is also noteworthy how well the instrumental section in this piece, including the Rachmaninoff quotation, flows together with and complements the rest of the song. This ability to fashion a lengthy piece with distinct musical sections into a track that sounds like a single, continuous, unified whole, with a satisfying balance between variety (from the differences among the different sections) and coherence (from the way in which they fit together and enhance one another) would become one of the band's trademarks.

'Sounds Of The Sea' 7:06 (Dunford/Thatcher)

This is the first Dunford/Thatcher composition to appear on a Renaissance album. (Many more would soon follow). Like McCarty, Dunford collaborated with Thatcher by mail, but in a different order than was the case with McCarty. Whereas McCarty would write music to fit Thatcher's lyrics, Dunford would instead send tapes of his music (and/or sheet music) to her, so that she could create lyrics that would fit his melodies.

This early collaboration, a leisurely-paced, piano-based showcase for Haslam's singing, has a musical structure that is much simpler and more straightforward than the typical Renaissance track (or Dunford composition), as it consists of three verses and three choruses, with no other substantial musical sections. Thatcher's lyrics are similarly straightforward, as they simply describe the joy of being near the sea, and of hearing its sounds. The song is framed, both at the beginning and the end, with tape-recorded sea sounds – especially the cries of seagulls and gently lapping, and occasionally crashing, waves. These 'sounds of the sea' are also intermittently heard in the background, throughout the track.

The arrangement is very spare, as if its main point were to provide as few sounds as possible that might distract the listener's attention from its proper focus – on Haslam's voice. In addition to the sea sounds and Tout's piano accompaniment, the only other major element is the harmony vocal on each chorus (by Camp, possibly in conjunction with Tout and/or Hendry). There is some rhythm section work, but both the bass and drum parts are minimal, are kept very low in the mix, and do not even make an appearance prior to the start of the second verse (with the drums barely noticeable prior to the third).

Haslam's singing here is notable, not only for its timbre and its expressive quality but also because it sounds very relaxed – an appropriate effect, given that the lyrics are about the pleasure of relaxing by the sea. And this sense of tranquillity, and of effortlessness, is evident even when she hits very high notes.

Following the third verse and chorus Haslam makes one more vocal contribution, in the form of some gentle, relaxed-sounding, high-pitched vocalise that is kept low in the mix – a fitting coda to this lovely, but rather slight, track. As she begins to fade out, the sounds of the sea, already present in the background, continue for about 30 seconds before they, too, fade out.

'Spare Some Love' 5:08 (Dunford/Thatcher)

Another Dunford/Thatcher collaboration, this one, like its predecessor, has a fairly simple structure – three verses, a repeated chorus, and a welcome interruption in the middle for a contrasting instrumental section. Thatcher's lyrics, which express the worn-out sentiment that in a world full of people who are lonely, and strangers to one another, there is a need to 'spare some love' and 'share your love', falls short of the standard she had set with 'Kiev' and 'Sounds of the Sea'. But Dunford's melody does not disappoint, and the potential monotony of repeated verses and choruses is averted by means of variations in the arrangement.

The track opens to the sound of Hendry strumming chords on his acoustic guitar. Haslam then enters with her lead vocal and sings the first two lyrical lines with no further accompaniment before being joined by the rest of the band.

While Haslam sings the verses alone, Camp harmonises with her on the choruses, and the rich, full sound that they make is one of the track's sonic highlights.

Following the second verse (in which the instrumentalists play behind Haslam from the beginning) and the second statement of the chorus, the band transitions to an instrumental break. It is set off by a brief passage in which Hendry, now on electric guitar, plays an ascending lick, which is perfectly synchronised with Camp's descending bass line and with Sullivan's drumming. This immediately gives way to another short episode, a drum and bass duet, which is, in turn, interrupted by an uncharacteristically harsh (for Renaissance) intervention by Hendry's electric guitar. The other players, as if stunned by the abrasiveness of his sound, drop out for a few seconds, as he plays his heavy rock lick alone. But then they come crashing back in, as Camp, matching Hendry's aggressiveness, plays loudly, and high up on the neck of his Rickenbacker bass (he sounds quite a bit like Chris Squire of Yes, whom he has cited as his bass-playing role model), while Tout offers a countermelody on top of the riff that Hendry continues to play.

The singers then return for another statement of the chorus, but this time the players drop out, and the chorus is rendered a cappella. As they sing, the absence of any other sounds very effectively spotlights the extraordinary resonance of their voices, making this the most enjoyable of the track's several iterations of the chorus. Moreover, the stark contrast between the blissfulness of this wholly vocal section and the excitement of the immediately preceding instrumental section establishes this entire middle part of the track as its clear highlight.

For the final verse, the band creates interest by making subtle changes in the instrumental backing to Haslam's singing. For example, Camp, playing quietly, uses a wah-wah pedal on his bass part, while Sullivan abandons his sticks and his drum kit in favour of hand drums.

For the final chorus, Sullivan returns to his kit, and Camp gives up the wah-wah pedal, while contributing loud, fast passages, high in his instrument's range, almost as if he were playing electric lead guitar.

At the conclusion of the chorus, Sullivan plays a short solo passage on cymbals as the track fades out.

'Bound For Infinity' 4:21 (McCarty/Thatcher)

The shortest, and slightest, track on the album, this McCarty/Thatcher collaboration nonetheless offers much to enjoy. Another showcase for Haslam's vocals, here she is supported only by the instrumental players, as there is no vocal harmony part during the song's three verses, and she harmonizes with herself (by means of overdubbing) on its lovely 'ba da da' middle section.

The vocal melody for the verses proceeds very slowly, thus bringing out previously unheard elements in her singing, as there are many held notes, often in her lower register, that she sustains at length, sometimes adding vibrato near the note's end. As usual, her singing is highly expressive, in this case conveying a tranquil, dreamy mood, in keeping with the lyrics which, like 'Sounds of the Sea', are about the pleasures of relaxing outdoors, near water, taking calm, unhurried comfort from the 'warm sun shining through seagulls wings', the 'mottled patterns' they make 'upon the sea', the 'salty glistening sheen' of the water, the ocean breezes, and the like.

The band's playing is appropriately restrained. Sullivan's drumming is especially noteworthy, as he plays quietly and unobtrusively, sometimes on hand drums. A particularly nice touch is Hendry's contribution, in which he uses his electric guitar to mimic the calls of seagulls.

But the highlight of the track is Haslam's vocalise part, in which she harmonises with herself while singing an ascending series of 'ba da das'. This beautiful section lasts less than 30 seconds, leaving one wanting to hear it repeated.

Indeed, if one were to criticise this track, it would probably be more for what it leaves out than for what it includes, as, very uncharacteristically for Renaissance, it also does not contain any extended instrumental sections. But the next selection more than makes up for that deficiency.

'Rajah Khan' 11:31 (Dunford)

Renaissance's third album ends, just as its two predecessors did, with its longest and most controversial track. It is by far the most complex piece on the album, and it is the one most in keeping with the style commonly referred to as 'progressive rock'. What divides listeners, aside from the length and complexity of the track, is its uniqueness – all the ways in which it differs from other Renaissance pieces. It has a harder edge, a more prominent use of electric guitar, and a more extensive use of non-western modes, sounds, and instruments (by turns, Indian and Middle Eastern) than any other Renaissance track. It is uncharacteristically menacing, so much so that, were it sung by someone with a voice much less sweet than that of Annie Haslam, it would not sound out of place on a King Crimson album. Finally, aside from 'Prologue', it is also the only piece in the band's catalogue in which all of the vocal parts are in vocalise, with no sung lyrics.

The strangeness starts at the very beginning. While several previous Renaissance pieces had opened with just one instrument playing a solo, in the past this had usually been a piano, and otherwise a gently strummed acoustic guitar. Here we get an abrasive, psychedelic, feedback-laden, dirty-toned, two-and-a-half-minute workout from Hendry. He plays freely, with several stops and starts, and makes no attempt to establish any kind of steady rhythm – all the better to frame and to serve as a contrast to, the rock-solid 4/4 beat that the full band establishes when it finally enters.

Haslam's vocalise makes its first appearance shortly thereafter, and she turns in a virtuoso performance, beautifully and powerfully delivering the song's non-western style melody with a wide assortment of vowel sounds.

The unusual harmonic pattern supporting her vocal is also noteworthy. Indian classical music is not constructed on the basis of harmony or chords, as these are conceptualised in connection with western classical and popular music. While Renaissance in this passage does not go so far as to eliminate chordal structure entirely, what can be said is that no chord *progression* is used during the first one minute and fourteen seconds of Haslam's vocal. Instead, the band just keeps bubbling and bouncing along on one chord, D major, creating something of a rhythmic drone effect. It is significant, in this context, that an Indian drone instrument, a tamboura, is played continuously during this sequence.

It is remarkable how varied is the melody that Haslam sings here, given that its background is so harmonically restricted. Indeed, her performance is so compelling that one might not even notice the drone, or the absence of a chord progression, on first listen. But the drone does finally give way to two chord changes as Haslam continues to sing, thus establishing something of a western-style chord progression in this otherwise eastern-sounding piece.

This progression quickly gives way, however, to a new section, in which Camp lays down an arpeggiated bass pattern, while Hendy plays clean, rippling, liquidy electric guitar lines quietly over an even quieter synthesizer background. But then, just thirteen seconds later, the players kick into full rock band mode, with Camp (once again) sounding like Chris Squire as he jacks up his volume for a thunderous bass riff, matched by an almost equally energetic Sullivan on drums, as both play in support of an insanely aggressive synthesizer solo by guest musician Francis Monkman of the band Curved Air.

Haslam and Camp shortly join in with vocals, harmonising on long-held notes sung in vowel-sound-based vocalise, as Sullivan, and even more so Monkman and Camp, continue to blast away in support. This gives way to a repeat of the first vocal section, in which the band plays a droning D major chord, complete with tamboura, behind Haslam's vocalise.

This, in turn, transitions to a new, brief, episode, in which Haslam (starting in the stratosphere) and Camp sing a descending four-note pattern four times, with the supporting players adding interest by changing their accompaniment, and making it progressively more complicated, each time this vocal part is repeated. Especially noteworthy is Camp's transition from a graceful, fluid, and rather melodic bass part on the first vocal descent to a hammering, rhythmic, unmelodic line on the third, with Sullivan joining in to play the same rhythm pattern on drums, thus intensifying it, and giving it an even greater sense of urgency.

This is followed by a new, heavy rock, section, as all of the players get a chance to blast away, with electric guitar, piano, drums and bass all taking a brief turn in the spotlight, amid the almost equally fiery ensemble playing. Hendry, on guitar, and Sullivan, on drums, both take brief solos, after which the most psychedelic episode in Renaissance's catalogue occurs. As the drum solo continues, Haslam's voice, sounding distorted and far away, as if part of some wild, troubled dream, gradually fades in, only to fade back out, and then back in again, several times. Soon the rest of the band drifts back in, also in a hazy, dreamlike way, accompanied by weird sound effects.

At about 9:08, the entire soundscape starts to slow down, before transitioning back to one more iteration of what might be considered the main section of the piece – the initial (and once repeated) vocal section. This time the Indian music influence is underscored even further through the incorporation of tablas, which are Indian hand drums.

When this concludes, we get a recapitulation of the heavy rock section that had been heard just prior to the psychedelic episode, during which the band simply stops, rather abruptly – a stunning ending to a mind-blowing track, and to a very promising first album from the new incarnation of Renaissance.

1. In order to distinguish precisely one note from another, it is necessary not only to identify the pitch (so as to distinguish, say, a 'C' from a 'B-flat'), but also the register (so as to distinguish a higher 'C' from a lower one). By a standard convention, middle C is designated 'C4.' An octave lower is 'C3,' while an octave higher than middle C is 'C5,' an octave higher than that is 'C6,' and so on. It is important to note that in this system each octave begins on C and ends on B. So, for example, the B that is seven steps higher than middle C (C4) is B4, not B5. B5 would be the note that is just shy of two octaves above middle C.

Ashes Are Burning (1973)

Personnel:
Jon Camp: bass, vocals, guitar
Annie Haslam: vocals
Terry Sullivan: drums, percussion, backing vocals
John Tout: keyboards, backing vocals
Michael Dunford: acoustic guitar
Andy Powell: electric guitar on 'Ashes Are Burning'
Richard Hewson: strings arrangements on 'Can You Understand' and 'Carpet of the Sun'
Producer: Dick Plant and Renaissance
Release date: October 1973
Highest chart position: 171 (US)
Running time of original LP: 40:42
Note: The 2019 Esoteric label reissue contains three live recordings as bonus tracks. These are discussed in a separate chapter devoted to live Renaissance recordings.

While the Renaissance line-up was by this time finally starting to stabilise, there was still continuing turnover at the guitar position. Rob Hendry, who had been brought in on short notice for the *Prologue* recording sessions because of the untimely death of Mick Parsons, departed soon after those sessions had been completed. Pete Finberg was hired to replace him, as the band toured extensively in 1973 to promote *Prologue*. However, by the time the band was ready to record its new album, *Ashes Are Burning*, they had decided to go in a slightly new direction, dropping electric guitar (almost) entirely, in favour of a more acoustic sound. One factor in this decision is that the band liked the sound of Michael Dunford's acoustic guitar when he, as the band's principal composer, would teach his new songs to his colleagues by coming into the studio and playing them on his instrument. Though Dunford still did not consider himself an official member of the band, since he was concentrating on composing, and was not performing with the band on tour, he agreed to supply some of the acoustic guitar parts on the album (with Camp contributing the others). Sometime after the album was completed, he did come on board as an official, performing member, but this happened too late for him to be credited as such on the album sleeve, or pictured with the other four players on its cover.

The new album also initiated a further sonic change, as the band, for the first time, incorporated orchestral playing into its sound, employing a small orchestra on two tracks, 'Can You Understand' and 'Carpet of the Sun'. With the dropping of the electric guitar (except for a brief passage on one track) and the addition of orchestration, the band moved even further away from a standard rock sound than it had done on *Prologue*, and also brought its classical influences more to the fore. Along with these changes, the songwriting skills of Dunford and Thatcher were steadily improving, and the band members, benefiting from the consistency of a relatively stable line-up, were becoming tighter and more cohesive as a unit – the unsurprising result of playing so much together on their rigorous touring schedule. Though *Prologue* had not been a big seller, it had been favourably regarded by most of those who heard it, and the band, playing the *Prologue* songs in concert, were developing a solid and loyal fan base. Thus, it was with increased confidence that Renaissance entered the recording studio in April 1973 to begin recording *Ashes Are Burning*, an album that would go on to be acclaimed even more highly than its impressive predecessor.

'Can You Understand' 9:49 (Dunford/Thatcher)

The leadoff track is an epic, multi-section, standout, and the first Renaissance recording to feature an orchestra.

It starts off with a bang – literally – as the first thing we hear is a gong. As the gong strike fades away, Tout enters with a piano melody, inaugurating a lengthy, piano-led, instrumental introduction. As he develops the theme, the other players, one by one, join in, beginning with Camp on bass, followed by Sullivan's drums, then acoustic guitar, then Tout's harpsichord, and then, finally, occasional electronic keyboard bursts from him, which he layers on top of his on-going piano part. As this section lasts about two-and-a-half minutes and is somewhat repetitious, some listeners might find it overly long. But the interest lies in the variations on the melody, and even more on the variations in the accompaniment, especially as the track builds in intensity, just pulsating along, with the normally restrained Sullivan rocking out on drums, and with Camp, his Rickenbacker bass mixed high, providing an aggressive, trebly, sometimes jabbing, other times bubbling, counterpoint to the more classically-inflected pianism of Tout. (Camp claims, in a 2012 interview, that he and Tout are the uncredited composers of this section.)

Another gong strike signals the end of this first section. After its decay brings the track almost to the point of total silence, voices, singing 'ah's in vocalise, quietly fade in, singing a new, eleven-note melody, and then repeating it, starting at a higher pitch, as their voices gain in volume. As they hit the last note in this sequence, a twelve-string acoustic guitar enters, gently strumming an alternating two-chord sequence (Ab and B), in a 3 + 3 + 2 rhythm pattern, so familiar to fans of the original Renaissance line-up, which is Haslam's cue to begin singing the song's opening verse.

At the conclusion of the first verse, the guitarist (either Dunford or Camp) reprises the eleven-note theme, initially stated in vocalise, on his guitar. He does so by strumming a new chord for each note in the sequence, where each chord is a major triad, the root note of which is the note for that part of the melody. In this way, the eleven-note melody also becomes an eleven-chord harmonic pattern.

Following the second statement of this progression on guitar, Haslam returns to sing the second verse, which is followed, in turn, by two more iterations of the eleven-chord acoustic guitar sequence.

The guitarist then switches to a new, alternating two-chord sequence, rhythmically more straightforward (no more 3 + 3 + 2) than the pattern he had used to introduce the verses, and is then quickly joined by a tambourine. This serves as the foundation for a new vocal section, in which Haslam repeatedly invokes the song's 'Can You Understand' title. At the end of its final iteration, she sustains its final note, powerfully, for a full ten seconds, during which the male singers join her with their own brief countermelody.

A new section then begins as Tout, accompanied by acoustic guitar strumming, launches into a new, very lovely, melody. And this beautiful section is also quite effectively arranged, incorporating sleigh bells (which add to the Russian flavour of the piece), drums, and, making their first appearance on a Renaissance recording, strings. The loveliness of the section is ratcheted up a few more notches when the orchestra comes in more fully, adding a string part high on top of Tout's continuing piano melody, while horns, operating unobtrusively at the bottom and mid-range, add yet another delightful element into this mix. Then, when Haslam returns to sing the final two verses, the orchestra sticks around, joining the band in accompanying her.

Before moving on, three comments about the section just described are in order, two of them positive, but one negative. On the plus side, the section flows together with, and complements extremely well, the material that both precedes and follows it, nicely illustrating the band's continually improving ability to compose and perform convincing, coherent, multi-section pieces. Furthermore, the integration of the orchestra with the band is completely successful. The balance between band an orchestra is good; neither one drowns out the other; there are no jarring timbral inconsistencies stemming from the juxtaposition of instruments that are not usually heard together, and the orchestral parts genuinely add something of musical interest, do not sound merely added on, and are not used simply to sweeten the sound of a 'rock' band. All of the pitfalls that are normally associated with attempts to merge an orchestra with any kind of non-classical musical ensemble are successfully avoided.

But on the downside, here Renaissance's deplorable habit of 'borrowing', without giving credit, from the work of other composers, finally catches up with them. The section just described is almost entirely the work of the French composer Maurice Jarre, from his score for the popular 1965 film, *Doctor Zhivago* (the particular piece in question is called 'Tonya and Yuri Arrive At Varykino'). As Haslam and Dunford both tell it, the band knew that the music was from the film score, but somehow were under the impression that this part of it was from an old traditional Russian folk song, legally in the public domain. Jarre sued, and the band had to pay a substantial sum in order to settle the case.

Back to the track. Immediately following Haslam's singing of the song's last two verses, the guitarist reprises the eleven-chord sequence that was first heard at the conclusion of the first verse. This time he is accompanied both by

Camp's bass and by the orchestra. While Camp's trebly, high-mixed bass line remains constant through each of these repetitions, the orchestral part changes each time, incorporating more instruments, and thus getting louder, each time the sequence comes around, with the strings also going higher and higher in each of the last three iterations. This is a polymetric passage, as the eleven-chord figure, which is in 11/4 time, plays against an accompaniment that is in 4/4. Sometimes the figure and accompaniment 'line up', but sometimes they don't, giving an unbalanced, swimmy feeling to the passage.

Then, defying the listener's expectation that an eighth rendering of the eleven-chord sequence is about to be heard, the band instead immediately launches into a reprise of the piano-driven opening instrumental section, this time enhanced by the presence of the orchestra. The well-integrated band and orchestra proceed to play an abbreviated version of this section (just over a minute), before concluding with a triumphant, expansive C major chord, which they hold for several seconds before the decay of the chord results in the track's final silence.

Three final observations about this piece: first, notice that the band incorporates the orchestra into this arrangement in a surprising way. Rather than having the orchestra play straight through, or in alternating sections, or perhaps in just one section especially suited to orchestral playing, the band chooses to play all of the main sections first without an orchestra, and then to reprise all of them, except for the middle vocal part (the 'Can You Understand' section), with an orchestra.

Secondly, to expand on the point that Camp often plays loudly, aggressively, and toward the high end of his instrument's range, this is a tendency that will only increase going forward – and I suspect that this is partly to be explained by the absence, beginning with this album, of electric guitar. Moreover, given Tout's preference for piano over electronic keyboards, Sullivan's spare, restrained drumming style, and now the presence of an orchestra, the jettisoning of the electric guitar leaves Camp's electric bass guitar as the one remaining rock element in the band's style. The fact that he is a highly-skilled, classically trained, player, fully capable of handling melodic or contrapuntal lines, coupled with the fact that Dunford's compositions rarely stand in need of a simple bass arrangement, helps further explain why Camp often plays more like a lower register lead guitarist than a bassist. The Chris Squire influence, already mentioned, is also an important factor here, as is the knowledge he gained from his experience as a lead guitarist in some of his previous bands.

The final observation is about Haslam's singing. On this track, it is as impressive as ever, and perhaps more so – controlled, powerful, pitch-perfect, expressive, and with a gorgeous timbre. She sounds more confident than she did on *Prologue*, and being still a relative newcomer to professional singing, had undoubtedly benefited from the experience of having made a previous album, and of having by now sung with the band many times in concert.

This is important, because the one sonic element that is most identified with Renaissance, and that most distinguishes it from all other bands, is the sound of her voice. As she had received classical voice training from an opera singer, it is unsurprising that her singing style is not in the rock tradition. But she also does not sound like an opera singer. Listeners who are more familiar with the (typically) untrained voices of rock or folk singers tend to find opera singing a bit pompous, overly stylised, and artificial. But while Haslam's singing is invariably clear and precise, it always sounds completely natural and unfussy.

And this is just one of several ways in which her singing successfully combines qualities that would ordinarily be in tension with one another. Somehow her singing manages to sound both free *and* controlled, powerful *and* soft, expressive *and* restrained. It is not that her singing exemplifies a kind of mushy, middling compromise among these different, seemingly competing, elements. Instead, each element is fully realised in itself, and also combines with each other one to create a unique *gestalt*. For example, her voice sounds powerful insofar as she sings with confidence, hits the notes squarely in the middle, and creates a thick, rich, full sound. And yet, there is a quality of softness in her voice as its timbre is devoid of harshness (even her very high upper register is not the least bit shrill), and as she seems to glide from note to note effortlessly, with no sense of the straining, yelling, bellowing quality that many opera singers exude. (Words commonly used to describe her voice include 'celestial', 'angelic', 'pure', 'crystalline', and 'soaring'.) Similarly, while she sings with extraordinary precision, both in terms of faithfully conveying the melody and in clearly enunciating the words, she does so without sounding robotic. Instead, there is a warm, human, unmechanical quality in her singing, as she fully engages, and conveys to the listener, the emotive content of both the melody and the lyrics she is singing.

She is a soprano, indeed, a 'coloratura' soprano, which denotes a singer with a very high range and extreme agility – an ability to handle difficult runs, leaps and trills. In many Renaissance compositions, she makes use of that ability by singing musical parts that contain no lyrics, hitting the notes with nonsense syllables rather than words, somewhat in the manner of scat singing in jazz. However, while scat singers generally use this technique in the context of performing improvised vocal solos, Haslam is more frequently singing a composed line. The absence of lyrics enables the listener to focus on her voice solely as a musical instrument, rather than as a conveyor of words. Also, in live performance, without an orchestra, but while performing a piece that had used an orchestra in the original studio version, she sometimes performs as a wordless vocal a line that had been played by an orchestral instrument on the recording.

There is no other singer quite like her.

'Let It Grow' 4:15 (Dunford/Thatcher)

This slight, unspectacular track is nonetheless thoroughly pleasurable, thanks mainly to its vocal melody, and to Haslam's performance in delivering it.

The structure of the piece and its arrangement are both quite simple and straightforward. A piano-led introduction leads into Haslam's vocals, wherein she sings three verses and follows each one with a rendition of the chorus. Following the completion of the lyrics, there is an elegant outro section, in which Haslam and the band's male singers harmonise in 'la la la' vocalise on a new melodic fragment, different from that of the verses or of the chorus.

The arrangement begins simply, as Haslam initially sings to piano accompaniment; but the other band members all, one by one, eventually join in, and their playing gradually intensifies as the track proceeds.

While all of the tunes (for the verses, chorus, and outro) are pleasant and well sung, Thatcher's words here are nothing special. In her defence, the song is about the joy of being in love, and there simply isn't much to be said on that subject that hasn't already been said a million times before.

A special highlight of the song is Haslam's leap up to an E5 note at the end of the first and third line of each chorus (on the words 'slow' and 'flow'). She has stated in interviews that Dunford made a point of writing specifically for her voice. I assume that this chorus is an example of that.

'On The Frontier' 4:53 (McCarty/Thatcher)

The only song on the album composed by McCarty, rather than Dunford, this is also an extremely unusual song in the Renaissance catalogue in that it technically qualifies as a cover version. It was originally recorded as the title track for the one album released by McCarty's short-lived band, Shoot, which, like *Ashes Are Burning*, was released in 1973. Comparing the two versions is instructive, for while Renaissance retains the lyrics and the vocal melodies found in the original Shoot recording, in almost every other aspect of Renaissance's arrangement the band plays to its strengths and departs significantly from its source material.

Whereas in Shoot's version the song is an electric guitar-based rocker, in which the entire band plays from the outset, Renaissance, taking the song at a slower tempo, ditches the electric guitar, and begins, as it so often does, with just one instrument playing, in this case, acoustic guitar. After the guitarist establishes the chord progression of the song's first section, Haslam and Camp, doubling each other an octave apart, begin to sing the first verse – another deviation from the Shoot version, in which a single vocalist sings the verses.

While the two Renaissance vocalists sing the first two lines accompanied only by acoustic guitar, the rest of the players – on piano, drums, and bass – then join in to provide backing for the remainder of the first verse and the entirety of the second. Retaining the song's original key, Camp sings the same notes as his Shoot predecessor. But Haslam, an octave higher, introduces a qualitatively new sonic element into the song, as when the melodic progression moves up a fourth on the third line of each verse she enters the stratosphere, reaching, at the highest point, a G5 note.

The weak link in the song, in both versions, is the chorus, which is first heard at the conclusion of the second verse. It consists of the line, 'We're on the frontier now', set to a somewhat clumsy, unmemorable, melody, which is then simply repeated a few times, without undergoing any kind of development, either melodically or lyrically. But Renaissance's arrangement does, once again, deviate significantly from that of the original recording – it minimises the impact of the chorus by the simple means of singing it less often. Whereas Shoot revisits the chorus twice following its initial statement, thereby singing its 'We're on the frontier now' line a total of fourteen times, Renaissance sings the line just six times, with five of those coming in the chorus's initial appearance. Having sung the chorus once, Renaissance brings it back only once more (rather than twice, as in the original), and then sings its one line just once (rather than repeating it multiple times in each reiteration, as Shoot had done). And as a final difference, Renaissance introduces some variety into its singing of this line by having the band drop out in two of the six instances in which it is sung, in favour of an a cappella rendition – something that Shoot does only once in its fourteen chances. (It should also be mentioned that Haslam and Camp harmonise on the chorus, and do not simply double each other an octave apart, as they do on the verses.)

Within ten seconds of the conclusion of the first chorus, Shoot, in the original recording, is on to the third verse. Renaissance, by contrast, takes well over a minute to get there, and only after inserting, first, a short instrumental section that has no analogue in the Shoot arrangement, and then its single, one-line, reiteration of the chorus, rendered a cappella. The instrumental section, consists of a short melodic fragment, introduced simultaneously on piano and bass, that is eventually joined, as the fragment is repeated, by wordless background singing (long, sustained 'ah's). Though the melodic fragment and the background vocals are both attractive enough, and though the band attempts to sustain interest by varying the instrumental backing throughout this short section, it still suffers a bit from the excessive repetition of the fragment itself, before the section gives way to the abbreviated reprise of the chorus.

The band then transitions to a much more successful instrumental section which, once again, bears no similarity to anything in the Shoot recording. Tout starts it off, establishing a classical-sounding theme on piano. But the mood shortly starts to change as Sullivan enters with a rapid-fire drum pattern, and is quickly joined by the guitarist, who inserts loud, crunchy, acoustic guitar chords, performed in a staccato rhythm that contrasts nicely with the fluidly continuous playing of Tout and Sullivan.

Somehow this serves as the perfect introduction to a different, seemingly unrelated, episode, in the form of yet another quotation from the classics, in this case, J. S. Bach's *Toccata and Fugue in D Minor*. Whereas Bach's famous composition is an organ piece, what we encounter here, is a dialogue, in a call and response pattern, between Tout's piano and Camp's bass. This leads us into the third verse, followed shortly by a return to the first two lines of the first verse.

The start of the coda begins just after four minutes in, a lovely, classical-sounding, descending chord sequence on piano, played a total of three times. The arrangement becomes more complex each time it is repeated, as Tout is joined, first by cymbals, then by finger-picked acoustic guitar, and finally by drums. Towards the end of the final descending sequence, the band slows down, signalling the end of the piece, which arrives in the form of a triumphant, sustained, Eb major chord, accompanied by a cymbal strike.

While Thatcher's lyrics are rather vague, they contain just enough specifics as to communicate that the 'frontier' in question is probably political and that the song is a call for solidarity in acting for change: 'We all are standing unafraid on the frontier.... / The day belongs to each of us our time is getting near... / So come on leave the dark behind and join the day now/ It's peaceful revolution time to join the day now'.

On the whole, despite the noted imperfections, this is still a good track with several enjoyable sections. If it is also the weakest track on the album, and perhaps the least successful one on any of the first five Haslam-era studio albums, that only testifies to the strength and consistency of the other material on those recordings.

'Carpet Of The Sun' 3:31 (Dunford/Thatcher)

The shortest track on the album, this stands as an exception to the general rule that the most highly regarded Renaissance tracks are the distinctive, multi-section, epics that clock in at nine minutes or more. For this fan favourite, and staple of the band's concert programs, has a simple verse/chorus structure, with no other significant musical development, and yet it is nonetheless loved and admired, simply for the beauty of its melody, and for Haslam's vocal performance.

Along with 'Can You Understand', this is the other piece on the album that features orchestral accompaniment; and, once again, this is done very successfully, as band and orchestra blend well and complement each other, with neither one at any time overpowering the other. This is something of an achievement since, if one listens analytically, focusing on first one, then another, instrument, one finds that they are all there, firing away, without much restraint – and yet, somehow, the playing does not sound busy, crowded, or loud. Instead, it comes off as gently supporting, rather than competing with, the main attraction – Haslam's voice – as it conveys Dunford's gorgeous tune.

Thatcher's lyrics are also enjoyable if one doesn't mind a slightly hippyish ecological vibe. Like 'Sounds of the Sea' and 'Bound for Infinity', here they are about the joy of beholding the beautiful sights of nature: 'Come along with me/ Down into the world of seeing/ Come and you'll be free/ Take the time to find the feeling/ See everything on its own/ And you'll find you know the way'. We are then enjoined to 'See the carpet of the sun', defined as 'the green grass soft and sweet', and also to 'Feel the sunshine warmth around you', and enjoy 'Sands upon the shores of time/ Of oceans mountains deep', while noting that they are 'Part of the world that you live in' and 'all part of you and me'. What makes this message about the value of the pleasures of the eye so convincing is that in receiving it, we experience pleasures of a similar kind – those of the ear.

As a final note, 'Carpet of the Sun' is unique in that it is the only Renaissance song for which one can compare Annie Haslam's vocal to that of her predecessor, Jane Relf, as a recording of Relf's performance of the tune (presumably a demo) is available on a two-disc CD compilation, *Jane's Renaissance: The Complete Jane Relf Collection, 1969-1995*. One of the points of interest in this recording is that it contains a verse that does not appear in the version that Haslam sings:

Come along and try
Looking into ways of giving
Maybe we will fly
Find a dream that we will live in
We'll look into the eyes of time
Past ages have turned to dust
And born somewhere on the line
The loving that grows with us

A reasonable conjecture as to why these lyrics were dropped is that they are not continuous with the ecological, beauties of nature, theme of the remaining lyrics.

'At The Harbour' 6:50 (Dunford/Thatcher)

Critics often claim to find a strong folk music element in the work of Renaissance in the Haslam era. So far as I can tell, however, the only basis for this claim is the band's preference for acoustic instruments. The melodies of Renaissance's songs owe very little, if anything, to any folk music tradition of which I am aware. Moreover, folk songs, however compelling they may be both melodically and lyrically, tend toward structural simplicity (just a repeated alternation of verses and chorus), in part to facilitate ease of communal singing by untrained vocalists. Renaissance's classic pieces, in quite radical contrast, tend to consist of multiple distinct sections, in the manner of multi-movement suites; to include lengthy instrumental passages; and to require the prodigious vocal talents of Annie Haslam, who effortlessly leaps from octave to octave with no loss of pitch accuracy. Moreover, journalist Jerry Gilbert reports that Haslam 'denies any familiarity or affiliation with folk music right down the line'; and, indeed, Renaissance sounds nothing like Steeleye Span, Fairport Convention, or Pentangle, perhaps the three most prominent British folk bands of the period, even though all three, like Renaissance, featured excellent female lead vocalists (Maddy Prior, Sandy Denny, and Jacqui McShee, respectively). Still less does Renaissance's sound resemble that of popular American folk groups, such as the Kingston Trio or Peter, Paul & Mary, or of solo folk singers, such as Woody Guthrie, Pete Seeger, the early Bob Dylan, Judy Collins, or Joan Baez (though Haslam, somewhat in contradiction to her statement that Gilbert cites, has repeatedly mentioned that as a young singer, prior to receiving voice training and joining Renaissance, she had greatly admired, and emulated, Baez's singing).

In any case, this is the track in which Renaissance comes as close as it ever would to doing a folk song. It is a haunting ballad that tells the story of a violent storm, a ship lost at sea, and women waiting, first anxiously, and then increasingly forlornly, for the return of the fishermen who, they fear, may have drowned.

The track begins with yet another uncredited classical quotation, as Tout, unaccompanied (except for a very brief passage on bass), plays a substantial portion of Debussy's piano prelude, 'La Cathédrale Engloutie' (The Sunken Cathedral). Debussy's piece is used to frame the ballad, as Tout returns to it to close out the track after the story has been told. It is an affecting, atmospheric, piece, but its connection to the ballad sounds a bit forced and arbitrary here – one of the few instances in which the different sections of a Haslam-era Renaissance track fail to flow together convincingly, so as to form a coherent whole.

Shortly after *Ashes Are Burning* was released there was a change in copyright law that altered the status of many early twentieth-century works, including Debussy's prelude. As a result, some subsequent releases of the album, and of compilations that included 'At the Harbour', edited out the track's opening and closing Debussy sections, leaving the ballad portion to stand alone. But more recent reissues have restored the track to its original, full-length, form.

There is not much of a transition from the playing of Debussy's prelude to the start of the ballad. Tout strikes the last Debussy chord and holds it, allowing it to decay. As it fades almost to silence, some gentle picking on a classical guitar emerges, with Haslam's vocal commencing just four or five seconds later. Haslam then sings the lyrics straight through, from beginning to end, in a two verses/chorus/two more verses/final chorus pattern, with no break for an instrumental section.

The arrangement puts all its emphasis on Haslam's vocals, as the instrumental backing is minimal throughout the piece, and always kept low in the mix. It consists of just classical guitar for the first two verses and most of the first chorus, with harmonium added at the end of that chorus, and both instruments carrying on, quietly, for the remainder of the ballad. The band deserves credit for this decision, as it must have been tempting to try to use all the resources at their disposal – booming drums, weeping strings, blaring horns, and so forth – in an attempt to bring out all the drama and pathos of the story. But as it turns out, the emotive content of the song is made all the more piercing by the arrangement's understated lack of bombast, as the combination of Thatcher's subtle, suggestive lyrics, a mournful harmonium, a pretty, just-sad-enough-without-overdoing-it melody, and, most of all, Haslam's gorgeous, evocative vocal, is more than sufficient for conveying it.

Perhaps the most affecting part of Haslam's performance comes at the end of the ballad when, accompanied by the melancholic harmonium, she sings:

Howling winds and the raging waves
Cracked upon the boats
And torn from safety torn from life
Men with little hope
Ghostly echoes at the harbour
Whispering of death
Women weeping holding hands
Of those they still have left

Shadows falling at the harbour
Women stand around
Weather storms another way
For men the sea had drowned

She reports that when she recorded her vocal, 'I sang in the stairwell because of the echo of my voice. We had people guarding the doors at the top and bottom of the stairwell to not disturb the recording'.

At the conclusion of the ballad, the track transitions, rather awkwardly, back to Tout's piano and Debussy's prelude, a section that lasts, just as the similar, opening section had done, one minute and 55 seconds. This time, however, there is an added element, as Haslam, for a substantial portion of this outro, adds faraway-sounding wordless vocals. Their faraway quality, especially in contrast to the upfront presence of her previous singing while delivering the lyrics, gives them a haunting aspect, further adding to the poignancy of this highly affecting track.

'Ashes Are Burning' 11:24 (Dunford/Thatcher)

With this album closer, Renaissance continues its unbroken four-album streak of saving its longest track for last. This time, however, there is no controversy over the merits of the closer, as 'Ashes Are Burning' is regarded, nearly by consensus, as a Renaissance classic. It would go on to become a fixture in the band's concert setlists, often serving as the encore, and also as the one song in which the band, which otherwise in live performance usually stays fairly close to the original studio arrangements, stretches out, improvises, takes solos, and alters and extends the piece, sometimes more than doubling its length.

This studio version begins with sound effects – wind sounds that gradually fade in, quickly to be joined by Sullivan's steady 4/4 rhythm on cymbals, which he first plays quietly, before gradually increasing his volume. Against this background, Tout's lovely piano melody then emerges, with support from bass and acoustic guitar shortly following. It is on top of this foundation that Haslam begins to sing Thatcher's rather vague, but poetic, lyrics, which appear to be about the need to let go of the past, so as to embrace the present freely.

Haslam sings all but one section of the lyrics straight through, without a break – two verses, then the chorus (in harmony with Camp), then two more verses (with Camp harmonising on the fourth verse – initially in contrary motion, ascending while she descends, then uniting in parallel octaves), and then a reprise of the chorus (again, with Camp). The vocal melody is memorable, and, as usual, Haslam's rendering of it only enhances its beauty. The backing instrumentation is light during the verses (with Sullivan mainly focusing on quiet cymbal work, Camp playing with restraint, and Tout's piano taking the lead), but much heavier during the chorus, with Sullivan attacking his kit, and Camp jacking up his trebly Rickenbacker.

At the conclusion of the second chorus, an acoustic guitar enters, playing a two-chord alternating pattern, high on the instrument's neck, in the by now familiar 3 + 3 + 2 rhythm pattern that the band favours. This sets the stage for one of Haslam's patented vocalise episodes, yet another pure, clean, lovely, soaring 'la la la' melody.

As Haslam holds the last note in this vocalise section, Tout, accompanied by Camp's high-in-the-mix bass, begins to play a short, transitional melodic fragment on piano. This leads to a short, but powerful, bass riff from Camp, signalling the beginning of a new instrumental section.

As Camp repeats the riff, playing it a total of eight times, he is joined, first by piano, then by harpsichord, then by drums, with each, upon joining, playing the same riff (or, in the case of drums, the same rhythm) in unison. The entire band then settles into a steady rock groove in 4/4, over which piano and harpsichord take turns in the lead, with the piano playing chord sequences and the harpsichord following suit, but playing the chords as arpeggios. Without breaking rhythm, the band then returns to Camp's short bass riff, which it plays twice, in unison, before moving up a step to play it twice more, but now in B minor.

As the band holds the last note of the last iteration of this riff, it shifts to a slower tempo and establishes a moody background (complete with celeste) for yet another memorable melody, this time played by Tout on organ. This organ solo gives way to a piano solo, which in turn, morphs into a brief full-band episode, with Tout now playing both piano and organ. This brief passage culminates in an eight-note ascending line, played in unison by Tout's harpsichord and Camp's bass.

Toward the end of that eight-note ascension, the band slows down, and then yields to the gentle sound of the organ, softly and slowly playing a repeating descending chord progression in E-minor. It is against this quiet, meditative, background that Haslam emerges to sing, softly and sweetly, the song's final vocal section. For the first eight lines of this melody, which is, yet again, an uncommonly lovely one, the accompaniment remains quiet and minimal, with no other instruments joining the unobtrusive organ. The first hint that a change is coming occurs next, following the completion of the eighth line, 'Ashes are burning the way', as guest musician Andy Powell, the highly acclaimed guitarist from Wishbone Ash, enters to sprinkle a few quiet electric guitar notes into the mix. We then immediately receive further evidence that something new is about to happen, as Haslam, who had not repeated any other lyrical lines during this section, begins to repeat the just-heard line containing the song's title. This sets up the song's climax, as she performs a thrilling variation on the melody at the end of this line. For this time, on the final note, she leaps up a major ninth, all the way up to a fortississimo E5, as in 'Ashes are burning the WAAAAAAYYYYY!'

As she holds and sustains this cleanly-hit note, the band kicks in, with Camp's bass and Sullivan's drums joining Tout as he plays a descending three-chord progression on organ, against which Powell launches into an electric guitar solo. The band then proceeds to jam on this progression at some length, with Tout varying his organ part, as Camp, in full Chris Squire mode, takes over the descending riff implied by Tout's chord progression. As the jam intensifies, Sullivan eventually begins to play a martial rhythm on drums, over which Powell continues his rather slow, but intense and expressive, solo. A bit later a celeste joins in, playing a repeating, ascending four-note riff as voices can also be detected, faintly in the background.

A little more than two minutes into the jam, the track begins a slow fade, which lasts the better part of another minute before the track arrives at its final silence.

Thus concludes the *Ashes Are Burning* album, in which this new version of the band moves a step up from the already impressive level it had reached with its first album, *Prologue*. But, by many accounts, its peak still lay in the future – the *near* future.

Turn Of The Cards (1974)

Personnel:
Jon Camp: bass, vocals
Michael Dunford: acoustic guitar, backing vocals
Annie Haslam: vocals
Terry Sullivan: drums, percussion, backing vocals
John Tout: keyboards, backing vocals
Jimmy Horowitz: orchestral arrangements
Producer: Renaissance, Dick Plant, and Richard Gottehrer
Release date: May 1974
Highest chart position: 94 (US)
Running time of original LP: 40:54
Note: The 2020 Esoteric label reissue, a 3 CD/1 DVD box set, contains many live recordings among its bonus tracks. These are discussed in a separate chapter devoted to live Renaissance recordings.

Following the completion of the *Ashes Are Burning* recording sessions, Michael Dunford agreed to join the band as a performing member. This put a stop to the revolving door at the guitar position and stabilised the Renaissance line-up, which would remain intact and unchanged until 1980, during which time the band would record and release 5 studio albums and one live double album.

The group continued to gain traction as a concert draw, especially in the north-eastern part of the United States, with the addition of the new *Ashes Are Burning* material adding to the band's appeal as a live act.

When they returned to the studio to record *Turn of the Cards*, the result of their efforts was a darker album, both musically and lyrically, than any of its predecessors, but also arguably the band's most consistent effort to date. With the electric guitar completely eliminated from the proceedings, they elected, once again, to utilise an orchestra on some tracks.

While the new album still failed to dent the charts in the UK, it cracked the top 100 in the US (a first for a Renaissance album), and stayed on the charts for 21 weeks. As three of its six tracks are dazzling, multi-section, symphonic epics, each running more than nine minutes in length, it is unsurprising that *Turn of the Cards* tends to be especially favoured by fans of progressive rock.

'Running Hard' 9:37 (Dunford/Thatcher)

The first of the album's three proggy masterpieces, 'Running Hard' has gone on to become a fan favourite and a fixture in the band's concert setlist.

Tout starts it off with a big, bold, majestic statement on piano as if to alert the listener to the fact that what follows will not be a light and breezy pop song, but rather a serious and substantial musical work – one that will demand and reward focused, attentive listening. Playing alone (aside from some brief assistance from Camp on bass toward the end of his solo), he quotes extensively (alas, once again without attribution) from *Litanies*, a

1937 composition for organ by French composer Jehan Alain. At first, Tout plays freely, frequently slowing down, speeding up, and occasionally almost stopping, before starting up again. But then, while still basing his solo on Alain's piece, he begins to establish a steady, 4/4, rhythmic groove.

Sullivan's drums make a bold entrance, signalling an imminent transition from Tout's solo to a full band episode. While remaining in rhythm, Tout responds by stretching out Alain's melody, holding each note longer than he had previously done before moving on to the next note (a device known as augmentation), thus making his musical statement take on an even more urgent and declamatory aspect than had previously been the case – an effect that is greatly intensified by the short, irregular, drum and cymbal blasts that Sullivan inserts to accentuate this brief passage.

All of the players then briefly slow down so as to spotlight the imminent arrival of the climax of this entire opening section – a triumphant striking of a C major chord.

Sullivan's quick drum fill then leads the band into the next section – the establishment of an up-tempo 4/4 rhythmic background, over which Haslam begins to sing the first verse.

The first two lines that she sings – and they are lines that lyricist Thatcher clearly means to emphasise, as they recur to serve as the first two lines of each of the song's three verses – foreshadow the compellingly beautiful darkness that will pervade so much of the *Turn of the Cards* album. Whereas in the closing title track of the previous album, *Ashes Are Burning*, Thatcher had written, optimistically, about the possibility of leaving the past behind (indeed, forgetting it), so as to move confidently forward into a bright future ('Your sins you won't remember/ And all you'll find there is love'), now the message seems to be that it is impossible to keep up with the fast rate of change in the modern world and that our desperate attempt to hold onto the world of the past, the one we had gotten used to, that we were comfortable with, and that made sense to us, is doomed to failure. The first words that Haslam sings are these: 'Running hard towards what used to be/ Losing ground in changes, sliding endlessly'.

While those two lines begin every verse, the third line of every verse starts with these three words, 'reaching out for...', and tells of an (always frustratingly unsuccessful) effort to grasp something out in that changing world that makes sense and provides comfort. Thus, the first verse ends, 'Reaching out for mirrors hidden in the web/ Painting lines upon your face inside instead'. Perhaps I'm over-interpreting, but I take this to refer to a failed effort to find a reflection of oneself in the world, so that, in order to fit into this world, one must instead artificially alter oneself.

At the conclusion of the first verse Haslam, with the orchestra now kicking in, moves on to the next vocal section (I won't call it the chorus, since it is never repeated.) Here we get more bad news. Twice we hear the phrase, 'sounds so bad', and once we are told 'you're dying all the time'. The section ends with these downbeat lines: 'Slipping through the day/ Lose the only way you know'.

Next comes the second verse, in which the tonal centre has moved up to A from the first verse's F#. Here, as always, we are 'running hard', but 'losing ground', just as we are also 'reaching out', but achieving bad results in doing so – in this case, 'Reaching out for things you want to see/ Find reflections of insane reality'.

Meanwhile, both the band and the orchestra, sounding very much like a single unit, continue to sizzle in the background, with trumpets, at the very end of the second verse, taking the lead in transitioning us to a new section, featuring Haslam's patented 'la la la' vocalise. With Tout's harpsichord now the most prominent instrument in the mix, the orchestra supports Haslam in her first reading of the 'la la la' melody, only to take over that melody when it is restarted, allowing Haslam to take a brief rest. When she then takes up the melody again, the orchestra first supports her but then drops out to make space for a brief vocal episode, in which Haslam and at least two of the band's male vocalists, with their voices staggered, each sing a different 'la la la' line, in counterpoint to one another.

At the conclusion of this section, cellos make a dramatic entrance, establishing a repetitive, insistent, rhythm pattern, soon to be joined by Tout's piano and Sullivan's cymbals. Shortly after this new section has been introduced, Tout, supported by the cellos, and by Sullivan's very rapid hi-hat pattern, plays a shapely melody that fans of earlier incarnations of the band will recognise as having been transplanted from 'Mr. Pine', the one Dunford composition to have appeared on *Illusion*. Sullivan testifies that it was Tout, rather than Dunford, who realised that this old 'Mr. Pine' fragment would fit in well here.

As this melody is repeated, a minor third higher, the excitement generated by this elevation of pitch is further intensified by the orchestra's energetic background playing (for example, note the urgency of the now higher-pitched cellos, as well as the new xylophone part). Next, Tout, continuing to play the melody, switches from piano to harpsichord, as the horns, woodwinds, and mallet instruments take turns supporting him. Somewhere along the way, the consistently present strings begin to double Tout, and finally to take the lead, in maintaining the melody.

The players then segue seamlessly into a second musical fragment borrowed from 'Mr. Pine', in this case, a majestic, ascending chord sequence, played mostly by the strings, with Sullivan bashing away on drums in support. (The chord sequence had been sung, in wordless, choir-like, fashion on 'Mr. Pine'.)

As this section reaches its climax, the orchestra plays, and holds, a triumphant D major chord. As it starts to decay, we hear Dunford, on acoustic guitar, starting to strum a simple, repeating chord progression. The starkness of this chord progression's contrast with the very involved and complex interplay of multiple instruments in the previous section helps to highlight the elegant simplicity of this very spare guitar sequence.

Then Haslam, now in her lower register, returns to deliver the third verse, with the tonal centre now having shifted to D (note that it is different in each of the song's three verses). The message is decidedly pessimistic, and this final verse ends with a particularly chilling final line: 'Running hard towards what used to be/ Losing ground in changes, sliding endlessly/ Reaching out for shadows passing through/ See the dark around is coming down on you'.

As she sings these lines, against the quiet background of Dunford's acoustic guitar, other instruments, such as bass and tambourine, slowly, and initially quietly and unobtrusively, begin to enter. But at the conclusion of the verse, this process begins to intensify. First Tout comes in to repeat the just-heard vocal melody on piano. Then strings enter, sometimes doubling him, sometimes soaring above, and eventually establishing a high harmony part. As more instruments join in (including drums and cymbals), and the playing gets louder, the martial character of the rhythm Dunford had established is increasingly felt. Then, the strings and horns begin to play a repeating descending countermelody against Tout's continuing piano re-statement of what had been the vocal melody of the final verse. The effect of this juxtaposition is magnificent – a fulfilment of the promise Tout had made at the beginning of the piece, with his bold, high-flown piano solo. The band and orchestra continue to play this striking, concluding passage for the better part of a minute, before a fadeout leads to its final silence.

The band's greatest strengths are all on display here. The piece includes several distinct melodies, all of them accessible, engaging, and memorable. Its many sections, which involve multiple twists and turns (changes in key, tempo, instrumentation, and the like), somehow hang together, flow into and out of one another smoothly, and come together to form a unity. The band and orchestra are well integrated. The lyrics are thought-provoking and affecting. The band's distinctive sound (piano, acoustic guitar, female voice, orchestra, no electric guitar) is firmly established. And Haslam's unique voice is present and in fine form. Little wonder that 'Running Hard' was chosen to be the album opener.

As Renaissance is also often called a 'progressive rock' band, and thus placed in the same category as such great bands as Yes, King Crimson, Genesis, Pink Floyd, Jethro Tull, and Emerson, Lake & Palmer, this track also brings out very clearly the major ways in which Renaissance is similar to, and different from, these other groups. Like all of them, Renaissance is noted for its classical influences, for its lyrical content that reaches far beyond the narrow range of topics dealt with in more mainstream rock styles, and for its challenging music that features lengthy, multi-section song constructions, and ambitious arrangements of instrumental parts incorporating interweaving melodic lines, instead of simple harmony.

But there are also important dissimilarities. Because it is relatively quiet, highly melodic, and features Haslam's beautiful voice, the music of Renaissance, more so than that of the major progressive rock bands just named, almost constitutes easy listening – or does so if one ignores the often rather dark lyrical themes. This difference in sound stems largely from the very different way in which Renaissance has borrowed ideas from European classical music. Unlike King Crimson, Yes, and Emerson, Lake & Palmer, for example, Renaissance has only rarely made use of those resources of twentieth-century modernism that lead to a harsh, abrasive, sound. Their classical borrowings are primarily from the highly melodic romantic era, and especially from the Russian tradition of Tchaikovsky, Rachmaninoff, Shostakovich, and Rimsky-Korsakov, rather than from the radically experimental, and often highly astringent, modernism of Stravinsky, Schoenberg, or Bartok. As a result, the music of Renaissance is, perhaps, more accessible than that of most other bands that are classified as 'progressive'. The compositions are 'catchable' on first listen, and are presented with less of the element of aggression that one finds in many major works of progressive rock. Often the pieces have a soaring, majestic, dramatic quality, with the drama sweetened by the beauty of the melodies and – to say it once again – by the unusually gorgeous timbre of Haslam's voice.

'I Think Of You' 3:07 (Dunford/Thatcher)

This short love song, which functions on the album as a kind of palate cleanser between the two long, intense, but otherwise very different tracks that precede and follow it, has a simple structure. Haslam sings three verses straight through, with no chorus, no substantial instrumental section, and, very unusually for a Haslam-era Renaissance track, no wordless vocalising.

Dunford starts it off alone, strumming chords on his acoustic guitar in the now familiar 3 + 3 + 2 rhythm pattern that he seems to favour, with Haslam's vocal commencing just ten seconds later, and the rest of the band joining in at 0:28. In contrast to the preceding track, the playing here sounds relaxed, with no sense of urgency. Haslam's singing is also relatively restrained, aside from a spectacular octave leap near the end of the third verse. The arrangement, too, is remarkably straightforward, with the most noteworthy elements being the introduction of harpsichord at the beginning of the third verse (it would take over as the lead instrument during the brief outro following the completion of the final verse), the band's sudden disappearance (which is obviously done to spotlight the just-mentioned Haslam octave leap), and the Sullivan drum fill that then brings the band back in. The orchestra is not used.

While it is difficult to say anything new in a love song, Thatcher takes a somewhat fresh approach here by associating the beloved person (the 'you' in 'I Think of You') with nature, as in the song's opening lines, 'I love you like a stream flows restless to the sea/ See you like the mist touches clouds, touches me', or its final verse: 'When I see a bird fly over to the sea/ And the sun in the sky is shining warm and free/ And when I feel the wind blow cool over me/ I think of you, think of you'. In this way she manages to incorporate her blissful response to nature, so evident in 'Sounds of the Sea', 'Bound for Infinity' and

'Carpet of the Sun', into the arguably worn-out genre of the traditional love song, directed to a person.

On the whole, 'I Think of You', while a pleasant, thoroughly enjoyable, song, stands as the slightest track on *Turn of the Cards*, and a minor work in the band's catalogue.

'Things I Don't Understand' 9:29 (Dunford/McCarty)

This is the second of the album's three lengthy, proggy, multi-section, classics, and the only song on the album for which Thatcher did not write lyrics. It is also the only song on *Turn of the Cards* for which founding member Jim McCarty receives a writing credit and the last song of his ever to appear on a Renaissance studio recording. It had not been newly written for this album, as Camp reports that the band had performed it live shortly after he joined, which was prior to the recording of the *Prologue* album.

This time it is drums, apparently a combination of Sullivan on his kit and another player on big, rumbling, orchestral drums (perhaps timpani), that kick off the track, with the orchestral drums starting quietly, but then rapidly increasing in volume. Then the band bursts in, laying down an up-tempo, syncopated groove to serve as a foundation for the impending vocal. Haslam and Camp shortly follow, singing the first verse together, an octave apart, before moving on to the 'Thinking about things I don't understand' chorus, where Haslam takes the lead, with Camp providing vocal harmony. This is immediately followed by the singing of the second verse and chorus, with the same distribution of vocal responsibilities.

While there is great value in spending time thinking about things one doesn't understand, this is partly because there are many important, deep, interesting topics that are at present either misunderstood or, at best, very incompletely and imperfectly understood. One can spend a lifetime thinking about science, art, music, or philosophy, without ever hoping to master, or exhaust, these subjects, and one can benefit greatly from the experience. But unfortunately (at least from my point of view), these lyrics appear to be referring to more dubious subject matter, such as astrology ('Stars that guide my destiny/ Tell me what I will be/ A chart unfolded') and predestination ('Seems there's plans for everyone/ The day will come and we will know').

In any case, the final note of the second chorus brings a change in both melody and harmony, indicating a transition to a new key. A new rhythm pattern and descending chord progression soon follow, and these serve as the foundation for a new vocal section – another uncommonly lovely wordless Haslam solo, in which she sings (sometimes with trills) 'la la la's and vowel sounds in the stratosphere. She then drops out, as the band's male singers, in unison, and doubled on harpsichord and bass, sing, an octave lower, the wordless melody she had just established.

At the conclusion of this episode, the band immediately transitions to the third verse, followed by the third chorus. Once again, it is during the latter part of the chorus that the band modulates to a new key, but this time, instead of waiting for the last note of the chorus to do so, as was the case with the second chorus, it happens with the chorus's second line. This, in turn, inaugurates a brief, piano-led instrumental interlude, which concludes, grandly on an E major chord.

As it gradually decays, Dunford enters quietly with a finger-picked acoustic guitar pattern, over which Haslam proceeds to supply yet another jaw-dropping, astonishingly high, vocalise solo. After going through this 'la la la' pattern once, the band kicks in; and for the second iteration, Haslam duets with her own double-tracked voice, which is shortly joined, rather subtly, by the band's male singers. Sullivan's drums come in more fully for the third iteration, as the band's playing grows in volume and intensity, and as the background singing in support of Haslam's lead also gets louder and more choir-like.

As this vocal section concludes, Tout, with band support, transitions to a lovely piano melody, the chord changes of which then serve as accompaniment to still another vocal section, in which Haslam and Camp, doubling each other an octave apart, sing a different melody than that of the verses, chorus, or any of the vocalise sections. In the second stanza of this section, with Camp now harmonising with Haslam, there is just a hint of political content, as the lyrics, written during the Vietnam War, speak of the need to 'hope and pray for peace'.

Following the completion of the sung lyrics, all of the band's singers immediately join together to continue this section in expansive, jubilant, vowel-based, choir-like vocalise, culminating, in another joyous E major chord.

As it decays, Tout takes over for the outro, playing chords on the organ, while simultaneously playing an ascending chordal melody on piano, toward the end of which he slows down and gently fades out, ending the track.

More so than the grandiose, orchestral, 'Running Hard', 'Things I Don't Understand' is a showcase for the band's vocal talents, as the singers successfully navigate multiple distinct vocal sections, handle both lyrical and wordless passages, incorporate solo, harmony duo, and multi-voice choir-like singing into a single piece, while also spotlighting Haslam's ability to sing absurdly high melodies, which she does without straining, with perfect pitch control, and without sacrificing any of the timbral beauty of her midrange.

The first side of *Turn of the Cards*, in its original LP format, opens with 'Running Hard' and closes with 'Things I Don't Understand'. It is rare to find two pieces of comparable scale and quality on one album side.

'Black Flame' 6:23 (Dunford/Thatcher)

The entire second side of the original LP is taken up with three moody, compelling, darkly beautiful tracks. This one, which leads off side two, features music that is ominous enough, and a Haslam lead vocal that is expressive enough, to fit in with lyrics that speak of 'screams inside the burning pain', and, repeatedly, of 'the black flame' that 'burns my blackened brain'.

The opening is minimalistic, with Dunford quietly picking out alternating D minor and G major arpeggiated chords on his acoustic guitar, accompanied by the occasional tinkling sound of bells or chimes, while Camp, playing high on the neck of his instrument, joins in on bass. The next to enter is Tout, first on organ, then, additionally, on piano, as the volume of the passage gradually increases. A little over a minute in, the band's male singers, in wordless, choir-like fashion, sing an ascending three-chord sequence a total of three times, in each case quickly yielding back to the band and a resumption of the song's original chord progression – the progression that will continue when Haslam enters to sing the song's first verse.

Toward the end of that verse, in which Haslam sings of having 'Lost the way in my confusion, in illusion/ Lost inside the picture frame', Sullivan comes in with a cymbal strike – a portent of the all-out drum attack, also accompanied by harpsichord, that will ensue as the verse ends and the song transitions to the chorus. As it does so, the song also moves from a 4/4 meter to the more irregular 7/4, as if to offer a musical illustration of the singer's 'confusion' and 'illusion'.

Thatcher has stated that in her use of the phrase, 'the black flame', written during the Vietnam War, she intended to refer to the way in which people can easily be persuaded to hate and kill one another – a phenomenon that the bloody history of war and genocide had shown to be present, very real, and seemingly ineradicable. The first line of the first chorus is especially potent: 'I'm not to blame, I didn't see the black flame'. While it may be true that large-scale murderous campaigns are initiated by powerful madmen, rather than by ordinary citizens, those campaigns could not be carried out without the willing cooperation of such citizens, who, perhaps taken in by patriotic, chauvinistic, and/or racist propaganda, fail to 'see the black flame', and subsequently console themselves with the thought that they are 'not to blame'. The unsquare meter helps to undermine such claims, as it conveys a feeling of instability and uncertainty. Those who are nonetheless taken in by the black flame are not merely victimisers, however, but also victims, who suffer from the corrosive effects of having allowed themselves to hate and kill (or to support killing), for the black flame not only kills the supposed enemy but also 'burns my blackened brain'.

Following the second verse and chorus, the band immediately transitions to a bridge, in which Haslam appears to take up the point of view of one who is hated by someone, presumably of another nation, race, and/or ethnicity, who wants to 'run from me', and to 'get away, any way'. In response to this would-be enemy, Haslam's character offers this response: 'Don't you see/ That we are one and I'm a part of you ... / I'm still a secret in the heart of you/ And I'm the burning in your soul'.

In this passage, starting on 'run from me', there's an effective use of a 'pedal', the compositional device where the bass note remains on one pitch under various chord changes, like a sustained organ pedal note. This device is used often near the end of baroque fugues, and frequently at the end of the development section (leading into the recapitulation) of sonata-allegro form movements in classical pieces, helping propel the music toward its conclusion. The pedal works in a similar way in this piece.

Toward the end of this section another wordless choir, rather low in the mix, gently fades in to back Haslam's lead vocal. When she hits the word 'soul', the final word of the bridge, she holds the note for twelve seconds, as the instrumentalists and the background choir perform a short transitional passage that leads, first, to an ascending chord sequence, performed without accompaniment by Tout on organ, and then to Dunford's reiteration of the acoustic guitar pattern that had inaugurated the piece – and that here signals the arrival of the third verse.

As that final verse arrives, to be immediately followed by the final chorus, we hear, once again, a hauntingly beautiful melody, conveyed by a spectacularly lovely voice (which sounds veiled here, after the major key brightness and excitement of the previous bridge), delivering an exquisitely devastating final message:

Now I'm weak, I am losing
I never thought I'd stop trying
I'm a lie, I'm just a sigh, just a crying
Just a symbol of the game

Suspended pain, I can not face the black flame
Intended fear, I can not trace the black flame
Extended reaching into space – the black flame
Burns my blackened brain

The gorgeous sadness is maintained in the song's final twenty seconds or so, which arrive at the conclusion of the final chorus. Haslam sings the word 'brain' and holds the note. As she does so, Dunford maintains his alternating two-chord sequence on guitar, as Tout and Camp, slowing to the finish line, perform a quietly sorrowful piano and bass duet.

'Cold Is Being' 3:00 (Dunford/Thatcher)

One might have expected Renaissance to follow 'The Black Flame' with a contrasting, cheerful, tune. Instead, the band chose to replicate, and, if anything, to extend and intensify, the atmosphere of desolate misery that 'The Black Flame' had so devastatingly established – and to do so with a song of similarly surpassing beauty.

'Cold is Being' is an unusual track in the Renaissance catalogue in at least two respects. First, it is one of the very few on which most of the band members do not play, as we hear only Tout's church organ and Haslam's vocal. Secondly, while Renaissance is notorious for incorporating quotations from classical music compositions into their own pieces, in this case, the entire song is simply an arrangement, for organ and voice, of Remo Giazotto's 1958 composition, *Adagio in G minor for strings and organ*, a famous work that is often mistakenly attributed to the eighteenth-century Italian baroque composer, Tomaso Albinoni. For the most part, Renaissance's arrangement just assigns the melody, which had been written for strings, to Haslam, who sings it with words that have been supplied for this purpose by Thatcher, though this new version reinterprets Giazotto's piece as mostly being in 4/4 time (the original is in 3/4), and simplifies it by leaving out many of his contrapuntal lines. (Since Giazotto wrote the tune, and Thatcher the lyrics, one wonders why Dunford receives a songwriting credit.)

Renaissance's version is short and straightforward. Haslam sings the lyrics straight through, in verse, verse, bridge, verse form, with her singing supported by Tout's big-sounding church organ, and with that organ also framing the singing with a very short (just eight seconds) intro, and a slightly longer, but still quite brief, outro.

As was the case with 'The Black Flame', Thatcher's bleak lyrics, and Haslam's emotionally charged singing, match the sadness of the song's melody. In the first two verses, Haslam sings:

So cold is being lonely
Behold the feeling lonely
The living part is done
The dying has begun
The world is spinning slow
So tired, slow

So cold is being sadness
Behold the feeling sadness
Oh how can we believe
We earn what we receive
The pain it overflows
Overflows

And the piece ends with these words: 'Stand quietly at the side/ Watch darkness open wide/ The light is growing dim/ So dim within'.

In reading some of the online commentary on *Adagio in G Minor For Strings And Organ* (for example, in discussions attached to recordings of it on YouTube), I found many statements to the effect that, because the piece is so beautiful, it shouldn't be considered sad. But being beautiful and conveying sadness are not mutually exclusive properties in works of art – a point that the ancient Greek tragedians well understood. In choosing to adapt this particular composition, and then in executing that adaptation with such intense feeling, the Renaissance band members show that they understand it as well.

'Mother Russia' 9:18 (Dunford/Thatcher)

'Mother Russia', the album's third proggy masterpiece, completes the dark sequence of its second side and closes out the album magnificently. (Its authorship is in dispute, as Camp, in a 2012 interview, claims that he composed 'most' of its instrumental sections.) The appropriately Russian-sounding piece, a fan favourite and staple of the band's concert programs, deals with the plight of a Soviet dissident, the writer Aleksandr Solzhenitsyn, winner of the 1970 Nobel Prize in Literature. Thatcher's lyrics are largely inspired by Solzhenitsyn's novel, *One Day in the Life of Ivan Denisovich*, which tells what life was like for a prisoner in a 1950s Soviet gulag. The novel had been based on Solzhenitsyn's own experiences, as he had spent eight years in a labour camp – his punishment for having criticised Stalin in a private letter (he would eventually be stripped of his Soviet citizenship, deported, and exiled).

Tout starts the piece off, as we hear a piano, sounding far away, quietly playing a minor-key melody. But the mood suddenly changes when Tout, with the microphone obviously having now been moved close to his instrument, strikes a loud, jarring note, accompanied by strings. As the note decays, we notice Dunford's guitar in the background, quietly picking a repeating lick on his acoustic guitar. A new minor-key melody then emerges, conveyed by a succession of orchestral instruments, including flute, at first, and subsequently violin. Swelling strings come in next with yet another melody, only to yield to the horns ten seconds later.

About a minute and a half in the orchestra begins to play, and then goes on to repeat several times, an ominous eight-note sequence, set to a rhythm that suggests rigid marching or stomping. This brief sequence is representative of the entire track in that it is very carefully, and effectively, arranged. With each repetition, the orchestra gets a bit louder, and the sonic mix a bit richer, as different instruments, at different times (horns, drums, xylophone) join in.

This passage reaches its climax at about the two-minute mark, as the orchestra strikes and holds its final chord. As it decays, the quiet sound of Dunford's acoustic guitar emerges and is quickly followed by the beginning of Haslam's vocal. With only acoustic guitar and a few quiet sweeps of harp strings, for accompaniment, she sings of a 'lonely man', internally exiled to frozen Siberia, who longs to return to his beloved home ('Cold as ice but he burns for you/ Mother Russia, can't you hear him too?').

At the conclusion of the first verse, the band and orchestra come in loudly, as a well-integrated single unit, to play, and then to repeat, an extremely catchy and emotionally potent four-chord sequence. At its conclusion, Haslam delivers the second verse, this time with the backing of the entire band, as Camp's bass and Sullivan's drums are especially in evidence. Following this, the repeating four-chord sequence returns and is then immediately followed by a bridge. Here Haslam further elaborates on Solzhenitsyn's sorry situation: 'Punished for his written thoughts/ Starving for his fame/ Working blindly, building blocks/ Number for a name'.

Next comes the repeating four-chord sequence, but this time it continues its cycle as the vocal resumes – Haslam and Camp harmonising on a new vocal melody, the first one to be based on the recurring chord progression just mentioned. Its concluding line is 'Mother Russia – he cries for you', with Haslam holding, and drawing out, the word 'cries', accompanied by rippling harp glissandos.

The conclusion of this vocal section leads to a lengthy orchestral section, in which a quiet, but insistent, martial rhythm is established, on top of which a succession of wind instruments, led by flute, but with colourful additions of bass clarinet and English horn, play a beautiful, melancholy, minor-key melody. Haslam, sounding far away, eventually joins in with some lovely, high-pitched, vowel-based, vocalise. As she repeats her melody, she gets progressively louder (but only slightly so), as the backing instrumentation (most notably guitar, harp and cymbals) also intensifies.

She then gives way to the orchestra, with Tout's piano initially leading the charge, accompanied by strings. Providing rhythmic support, Dunford and Sullivan persist in maintaining the martial pattern they had already established, as the ensemble playing continually increases its volume. An oboe eventually takes over the melody, with the horns subsequently joining in with a countermelody – as the volume and intensity of the playing increases, and the insistent quality of the marching rhythm (with the snare drum now replacing the sixteenth notes of the martial rhythm with triplets), also continues to rise.

The strings, at the top of the mix, then take the lead as they usher in the band's vocalists, who take up a repeating, wordless 'bah dah dah dah pattern eight seconds later. The final 'dah' in this pattern is sung as a G major chord in each iteration, except for the last one, which concludes a major third higher on a surprising B major chord.

This leads to the immediate return of the 'Punished for his written thoughts' section, followed, as before, by the repeating four-chord sequence, and then, with the band and orchestra firing away at maximum volume, by the vocal section that is based on it. As Haslam sings the word 'cries' in the song's final lyrical couplet ('So cold, so true/ Mother Russia – he cries for you'), players start to drop out, allowing her to deliver the final, poignant, 'for you' softly, over a relatively quiet background. She holds the 'you' note for eight seconds, as a flute plays a final, sorrowful, achingly beautiful, melody over Tout's slow, mournful piano accompaniment. As strings quietly sob in the background, the track then slows to its final conclusion, a B minor chord, which is allowed to fade to the track's ultimate silence.

Continuing its unbroken tradition of ending every album with an epic track (although here, for the very first time, not the longest on the album, as 'Mother Russia' is a few seconds shorter than both 'Running Hard' and ' Things I Don't Understand'), *Turn of the Cards* thus concludes on one of the high points of the entire Renaissance catalogue. With its three lengthy classics, two more very highly-regarded, moody tracks, and only one second-tier piece (and a brief one at that, at just over three minutes in length), it is one of the major candidates for the title of the band's best album, favoured especially by those with a taste for music on the dark side, and who appreciate the maintaining of a consistent emotional tone across the entire length of an album. Haslam, clearly reluctant to name a definitive favourite, is nonetheless willing to say that *Turn of the Cards* is 'arguably our most powerful record, with such a depth to the music and the performances'.

Still, were a poll to be taken, I suspect that the honour would not go to *Turn of the Cards*, but rather to its immediate successor.

Related Tracks
'Everybody Needs A Friend' 3:48 (Andrew Powell/Ted Turner/ Martin Turner/Steve Upton)

A bonus track on the 2020 Esoteric label reissue, this is a cover of a Wishbone Ash song, from their 1973 album, *Wishbone Four*. Renaissance had formed something of a relationship with that band, probably stemming from the fact that they shared a manager, Miles Copeland. Andy Powell, one of the writers of this song, had appeared on a Renaissance track as a guest artist, playing electric guitar on 'Ashes Are Burning'.

The original Wishbone Ash version, a mid-tempo ballad about the importance of friendship, clocks in at over eight minutes, as the band surrounds its three verses with extensive instrumental sections. Renaissance, largely foregoing those instrumental parts, reduces the song to less than half its original length.

It's easy to see why this track was left off the album. It doesn't fit the band's style (no evident classical influence, and no twists and turns in the song's construction), its mood isn't consistent with that of the rest of the album (too uplifting), and it just isn't as good a piece of music as anything that did end up making the cut. Haslam delivers a fine lead vocal, bit the material doesn't give her a chance to take off and soar.

Other bonus tracks on this reissue include the single edit of 'Mother Russia' (a hideous mutilation of a classic, done without the band's knowledge or consent), new stereo mixes of 'Things I Don't Understand, 'Black Flame', and 'Mother Russia', 5.1 Surround Sound and high-resolution stereo mixes of the entire album, and several live recordings. The live recordings are discussed in a separate chapter.

Scheherazade And Other Stories (1975)

Personnel:
Jon Camp: bass, vocals, bass pedals
Michael Dunford: acoustic guitar, backing vocals
Annie Haslam: vocals
Terry Sullivan: drums, percussion, backing vocals
John Tout: keyboards, backing vocals
Tony Cox: orchestral arrangements
London Symphony Orchestra
Producer: David Hitchcock and Renaissance
Release date: August 1975
Highest chart position: 48 (US)
Running time of original LP: 45:40
Note: The 2010 Friday Music label reissue includes a bonus DVD, ***Renaissance Filmed at Mill House and Bray Studios, 1979***, which contains videos of five Renaissance songs. These are discussed in a separate chapter devoted to Renaissance live and video releases.

With their *Turn of the Cards* line-up still intact, Renaissance returned to the studio in May 1975 to record *Scheherazade and Other Stories* – the sixth Renaissance album, and the fourth of the Haslam era. It would be the first Renaissance album to include no writing contribution from any of the band's original members, the first on which Tout and Camp would receive writing credit, and the first to contain no quotations from classical compositions. Though it failed to chart in the UK, it was the first Renaissance album to crack the top 50 in the US, as the band, building on the momentum of *Turn of the Cards*, which had been the first Renaissance album to reach the top 100 in the US, focused on expanding its American fan base through constant touring.

Featuring one piece that would take up an entire album side, and another that would clock in at just under eleven minutes, the new album would contain only four tracks – the fewest on any Renaissance album, before or since. But all four tracks would go on to be highly regarded, making the album probably the most acclaimed, by critics and fans alike, in the entire Renaissance catalogue.

'Trip To The Fair' 10:48 (Dunford/Thatcher/Tout)
Haslam has often told the story of how this, perhaps the most surrealistic song that Renaissance had ever done or would do, originated. She had gone on a date with the musician Roy Wood. After a late dinner, they had decided to visit a local fair. However, when they arrived at the fairgrounds, they found it to be empty of people, as the fair was closed – which should not have been surprising since they had not decided to leave for the fair until around midnight.

Haslam, finding the whole experience humorous, shared the story with her friend, Betty Thatcher, the band's lyricist, who decided to turn it into a song. But Thatcher altered the story so as to make it menacing, removing from the narrative both the protagonist's companion and the perfectly rational explanation for the deserted fairgrounds. Thus, a charming little story, about a strong, healthy couple making an innocent and harmless mistake, is transformed into a *Twilight Zone*-style nightmare, in which a solitary woman finds herself lost, abandoned, and seemingly somehow trapped in a frightening situation: the noisy crowds of happy people that should be present have inexplicably vanished, and she must face the possibility of becoming the next victim of the malevolent force (whatever that may be) that had made them all disappear.

Composers Dunford and Tout (the latter receiving his first Renaissance songwriting credit here) do a fine job of providing music that fits the claustrophobic and paranoid mood of such a story, as their composition has a dreamlike, hallucinatory, quality, as well as an aspect of looming danger. These effects are further enhanced by the song's production, which features a variety of odd and mildly disturbing noises and sound effects. There is no other Renaissance piece quite like it.

Tout starts it off alone, with an extended piano solo. Focusing on his instrument's lower register, he initially plays freely, before settling down to establish a steady 4/4 rhythm and a recurring melody – a cue for Camp and Sullivan to join in, which they shortly do.

Several voices (Haslam, multi-tracked for a choir-like effect) then gradually fade in, singing wordless 'ah's. The voices sound far away, not present, thus creating the disturbing sense that one is hearing voices without being able to locate their source. (Are the voices just in my head? Or do they belong to sinister entities, lurking in the shadows, preparing their attack?) A bit later, the voices having temporarily disappeared, we start to hear similarly distant, disembodied, laughter. And while laughter might be an appropriate sound for a carnival, this laughter has a mocking, mildly threatening, quality, rather than a joyous one – an effect that is enhanced when the laughter is quickly joined by the return of the eerie, faraway, singing.

Tout, continuing his piano solo, then enters into a syncopated duet with Sullivan, in the 3 + 3 + 2 rhythm pattern that the band so much favours, before switching to a 5/4 time signature, with Camp and Sullivan accentuating each downbeat. He subsequently changes yet again, sliding into 6/4 time, before yielding to a celeste, which creates a dreamy, music box, sound, suggestive of a carnival atmosphere. The celeste, as in 'celestial', is often used to suggest something supernatural, and it is used very effectively in that way in this piece.

Shortly thereafter Haslam enters, accompanied solely by the celeste, to deliver the song's first verse ('I took a trip down to look at the fair/ When I arrived I found nobody there/ It seemed I was all alone/ Must be that they've all gone home') and chorus (the line, 'A trip to the fair but nobody was there', sung twice).

In the second verse, as Camp's bass and Sullivan's drums quietly join in, Haslam sings, 'I wonder just what it means/ Is everything how it seems?', thus giving us the first hint of her realisation that this situation might not be real, but rather a hallucination. As she sings these lines, Camp establishes a suitably unbalanced accent pattern, as he plays a bass note on each of the first two beats of each measure, while resting on its last four.

In the third verse, the entrance of a calliope further establishes the sound and feel of a fairground; and threatening forces, whether real or imagined, come out of the shadows, as inanimate objects spring into action ('dodgems' are what are also known as 'bumper cars'): 'A creak as the dodgems came onto the scene/ Wheels began turning I started to scream/ A carousel swung around/ My head spun and hit the ground'. And yet, even after sustaining this attack, Haslam, reiterating the chorus, continues to insist that 'nobody was there'. Throughout this verse and chorus Camp perpetuates the off-kilter accent pattern he had established in the second verse by continuing to emphasise only the first two of six beats in each measure, even though he no longer rests during the remaining four.

Immediately following the third chorus the band transitions to a bridge, in which Haslam, conveying vulnerability, confesses her terror, while leaving it as an open question whether the threat is really external, rather than purely internal: 'I close my eyes to disguise the fear from inside/ Trembling within my own mind I find no place to hide/ Stars of tomorrow shine through the grey mist that has gone/ I wish that this trip to the fair had never begun'.

As she reaches the end of the bridge, Haslam holds onto its final syllable for ten seconds, melismatically turning it into an eleven-note phrase. After pausing for one second to take a breath, she then immediately repeats the phrase, sung while holding an 'ah' sound, without interruption, for fifteen seconds, as Camp joins in with a harmony vocal. Throughout both iterations of this melismatic fragment, the band abandons its asymmetrical backing pattern, with Camp and Sullivan, in particular, banging away throughout each measure.

The band then segues into a light, breezy, very jazzy instrumental section, in which the celeste and piano take turns soloing, in a back-and-forth pattern. Sullivan's drumming deserves special mention here, as he shows himself to be a very capable jazz drummer. One would think that an episode of carefree, relaxed jazz playing would sound jarring in this context, perhaps wrecking the entire track, as its mood is so far removed from the feeling of strangeness, confusion, and creeping terror that had pervaded the piece until now. But somehow, perhaps because of the presence of the celeste, with its supernatural connotations, it doesn't. It seems to fit right in, and one has no difficulty in enjoying it on its own terms.

About a minute into this jazz section distant, choir-like voices emerge, once again singing wordless 'ah's, but this time not sounding particularly menacing as they do so. The voices then give way to a return of the 5/4 passage, which now takes on a kaleidoscopic aspect, as it is played, not on piano, as it was before, but on harpsichord and celeste, and punctuated with loud cymbal and drum strikes. This signals the return of the calliope, the carnival atmosphere, and a verse, in this case, the fourth.

Right: The original Renaissance lineup. From left to right: Keith Relf, Jim McCarty, Jane Relf, John Hawken, and Louis Cennamo.

Left: The *Ashes Are Burning* lineup: Terry Sullivan, Annie Haslam, Jon Camp, and John Tout. Michael Dunford had not yet officially joined.

Right: The 2015 lineup: Annie Haslam, Tom Brislin, Leo Traversa, Frank Pagano, Mark Lambert, and Rave Tesar.

Left: The first Renaissance album, released in 1969. (*Island / Elektra*)

Right: The 1971 follow-up, *Illusion*. (*Island*)

Right: 1972's *Prologue*, the first album with an entirely new lineup, featuring the lead vocals of Annie Haslam. (*Sovereign*)

Left: 1973's *Ashes Are Burning*, featuring Annie Haslam and Terry Sullivan on the cover. (*Sovereign*)

Above: Former Yardbird Keith Relf, singing 'Kings And Queens' on the German television show *Beat Club* in 1970.

Below: Keith's sister, Jane Relf, adding her vocals to 'Kings And Queens' at the same gig in Germany.

Above: The first line up featured Louis Cennamo on bass and Jim McCarty on drums.

Below: John Hawken adds his classical flourishes on piano.

Left: 1974's *Turn of the Cards*, a darkly beautiful album, featuring three proggy epics. (*BTM / Sire*)

Right: 1975's *Scheherazade and Other Stories*, featuring just four pieces, including the nearly 25-minute side-long title track. (*BTM / Sire*)

Right: 1977's *Novella*. No, that's not Annie Haslam on the cover. (*Warner Bros / Sire*)

Left: 1978's *A Song for All Seasons*, featuring the top-ten hit single, 'Northern Lights.' And no, that's not Annie Haslam on the cover, either. (*Warner Bros / Sire*)

Left: John Tout at his bank of multiple keyboards, as Annie Haslam looks on. From the BBC *Sight and Sound* programme in 1977.

Right: The band's principal composer, Michael Dunford, playing his acoustic twelve-string guitar on *Sight and Sound*.

Left: Annie Haslam sings at the same concert.

Right: Jon Camp, playing high up on the neck of his Rickenbacker bass, as a seated Michael Dunford picks his acoustic guitar.

Left: Annie Haslam, singing 'Northern Lights' on *Top of the Pops* in 1978.

Below: Haslam, Sullivan, and Camp on the *Sight and Sound* program, the highest quality video recording of the classic mid-70s era Renaissance.

Left: *Azure D'Or* from 1979, the first of the band's three attempts to move in the direction of contemporary pop music trends. (*Warner Bros / Sire*)

Right: 1981's *Camera Camera*. With the departure of Tout and Sullivan, only Camp, Dunford, and Haslam are seen on the cover. (*Illegal / IRS*)

Right: Dunford, Haslam, and Camp on the cover of 1983's *Time-Line*. The attempt to stay current, evidently extends to hairstyles, in addition to the music. (*Illegal / IRS*)

Left: After an eighteen-year hiatus, Renaissance returned, with Dunford, Haslam, Sullivan, and Tout reuniting on 2001's *Tuscany*. (*Giant Electric Pea*)

Above: Dunford (centre stage) and Haslam, in the 2011 version of the band, performing the *Scheherazade* album.

Right: From the same concert, bassist David Keyes and keyboardist Jason Hart join Haslam and Dunford.

Rave Tesar on keyboards, live at Union Chapel, 2015.

Right: Annie Haslam and Mark Lambert at Union Chapel.

Below: Mark Lambert and Leo Traversa at the same gig.

Below: The band in full flight at Union Chapel. At the far right, on keyboards, is Tom Brislin, who has toured with Yes, and who is now a member of Kansas.

Left: The band's first live album, 1977's two-disc *Live at Carnegie Hall*, featuring a 24-minute version of 'Ashes Are Burning.' *(BTM / Sire)*

Right: The band's most recent live album, 2018's *A Symphonic Journey*, a video/double audio release of a 2017 concert. *(Symphonic Rock / Red River)*

Left: *Live at the Union Chapel*, a 2016 video/digital audio release of a 2015 concert. *(Symphonic Rock / Red River)*

Right: *Da Capo*, a two-disc retrospective of Renaissance's career to the 1980s. (*Repertoire*)

Left: The first volume of *Tales of 1001 Nights*, a two-disc 'Best of' compilation, which focuses exclusively on the band's prime 1970s output. (*Warner Bros / Sire*)

Right: The second *Tales of 1001 Nights* disc. (*Warner Bros / Sire*)

Left: *Grandine il Vento*, the band's 2013 studio album, in which Renaissance makes a partial return to its 1970s progressive rock style. (*Symphonic Rock / Red River*)

Right: Featuring an Annie Haslam painting on the cover, 2014's *Symphony of Light* is a re-release, with three bonus tracks, of *Grandine il Vento*. (*Symphonic Rock / Red River*)

Below: Annie Haslam, in a still from the video for 'Cry to the World,' a track from *Grandine il Vento*. The song features Ian Anderson of Jethro Tull on flute.

At this point the story takes an unexpected turn: 'Suddenly thousands of faces I see/ Everyone seemed to be staring at me/ Clowns laughed in the penny arcade/ What was this game my mind played?' As it seems highly unlikely that thousands of fair-goers could have suddenly returned all at once, this leaves us to wonder whether they had really been there all along, marking the earlier perception that no people were present as some sort of delusion, or was it rather that no one is here now, and the present perception of 'thousands of faces' is hallucinatory? Indeed, 'What was this game my mind played?'

Haslam appears to resolve the dilemma in favour of the second alternative, as she immediately resurrects the first verse, with its declaration that upon arriving at the fair, 'I found nobody there'. However, the sense of shadowy danger, and of mental breakdown, is further enhanced here by the presence of a loudly whispering voice, Haslam's own, doubling her in a ghostly fashion as she sings the verse. When she then transitions to the chorus, the whispering stops, but instead, she echoes herself, as her double-tracked voice, seemingly mocking her, repeats her 'nobody was there' line right back to her each time she sings it.

At the conclusion of the final chorus, the calliope-led background continues on its own for some time before the band's singers take up the on-going theme, singing 'ah's in faraway vocalise. Shortly after they do, the track begins a slow fade that ultimately leads to its final silence.

And the darkness, so characteristic of *Turn of the Cards*, continues.

'The Vultures Fly High' 3:07 (Dunford/Thatcher)

While very few of Renaissance's short tracks can plausibly be ranked among the band's best, this succinct, straight-to-the-point piece is one that can.

Rather than starting with just one instrument, and then gradually layering the rest of them in, one at a time, as Renaissance so often does, here the full band comes out blazing, right from the start, with Camp's bass and Sullivan's drums leading the charge. The intro is fast and edgy, and its nervous excitement is enhanced by the occasional slipping of single bars in 3/4 time into what is mostly a rocking 4/4 beat.

At just twelve seconds in, Haslam enters with her lead vocal. As befits the tempo, and Dunford's punchy C-minor melody, her singing here is unusually crisp, as she delivers Thatcher's withering broadside against the 'vultures'.

The song unfolds straightforwardly: first verse/chorus (with one of the harmony singers joining Haslam)/second verse/repeat chorus/key change for a short, but extremely tuneful, Tout synthesizer solo/repeat chorus/and final chorus (on which the song fades out).

But who, exactly, are the vultures? One possibility is that they are professional critics, perhaps those who would criticise a symphonic rock band, like Renaissance. (In a 2011 concert recording, Dunford endorses this interpretation.) On this reading, one can almost hear the pain in Haslam's voice, as she sings, 'It doesn't matter how you try/ It doesn't matter what you say/ They always watch with hollow eyes/ To put you down/ They always find a way to criticise'.

There are problems with this theory, however. For one thing, Renaissance tended to receive reasonably respectful treatment from the critics and were generally spared the scathing denunciations that some of the other progressive rock bands, such as Yes or Emerson, Lake & Palmer, had to endure. And Thatcher, in particular, the writer of these lyrics, had seldom been subjected to critical abuse. Moreover, Thatcher has revealed in interviews that the song had originally not even been intended for Renaissance, but rather for Wishbone Ash, another band that had not especially been targeted by music critics.

But the biggest problem is that the second verse does not seem to pertain to critics at all. So another possibility is that the ones who 'always find a way to criticise' are, in this song, the rich and powerful in society, and, especially bosses, rather than critics. The second verse, with such lines as 'Though you haven't much to give/ You know they take it, yours and mine', fits that interpretation, as do such lines as these, from the first verse: 'They reign supreme as orders go/ They are the last to have their say/ And last to know'. Notice that the boss makes the final decision, and thus has the final say, in spite of often not having as much knowledge relevant to the decision as do the employees who are actually on the ground, doing the work – hence, 'the last to know'. Also, vultures are opportunistic scavengers that avoid the hard work of killing healthy prey, preferring to take advantage of the killing and wounding work that other animals or people have done (for example, vultures have often been seen in abundance on battlefields, dining on the dead carcasses of soldiers). The vulture metaphor, in its aspect of ruthlessly exploiting the work of others, and of profiting from work that kills, applies more readily to bosses, and to the wealthy class more generally, than it does to rock music critics ('The vultures fly high/ They circle over us all'). That's my best guess regarding the interpretation of the lyrics. I could be wrong!

In any case, this song about vultures, whoever they might be taken to be, surely qualifies as yet another in the band's on-going string of dark tracks. And musically it sizzles from start to finish, with the aggressive playing of Camp and Sullivan, along with Tout's soaring synthesizer, perfectly complementing Haslam's impassioned vocal.

'Ocean Gypsy' 7:05 (Dunford/Thatcher)

The first side of the original LP closes with this beautiful, poignant ballad, a classic in the Renaissance catalogue, and a fixture in their concert setlists.

The idea for the song came to Thatcher after she had once witnessed the simultaneous rising of the sun and setting of the moon at dawn as she looked out over the sea from her home in Cornwall. She then imagined the sun and moon as frustrated lovers, unable to meet, and thus destined to remain alone forever. While the moon, the 'Ocean Gypsy' of the song's title, longs to be with the sun, when he appears, 'the ocean calls her'. Subsequently, we learn that

'Day has taken her and now she's gone'. The stars 'smile sadly for her where she falls', and, at the song's climax, 'Oceans weep for her, the ocean sighs'.

Haslam's vocal performance (joined by Camp's harmony on the chorus) hits the mark perfectly, in that it warmly conveys sympathy without falling into the trap of sounding excessively sentimental. She tells the story clearly, and with feeling, but mostly lets Thatcher's lyrics and Dunford's lovely, melancholic melody in A minor do most of the work of conveying the song's emotive content.

Surprisingly, given its length, this track, like its immediate predecessor, features a straightforward, verse/chorus construction (three of each, with an excellent piano solo and choir vocalise break following the second chorus), without any additional twists and turns.

The orchestra makes its first appearance on the album on this song, but it rarely comes to the forefront of the arrangement and is instead mainly used to provide gentle backing to the band's playing and singing. Given the presence of the orchestra, the persistent use of a synthesizer, also in the background, seems a bit redundant – a reasonable choice for a concert performance without an orchestra, but unnecessary here, and also arguably a bit of a negative, in that it introduces a cold sound associated with high technology into a track that otherwise sounds very warm and human.

'Ocean Gypsy', and, indeed, the entire first side of *Scheherazade and Other Stories*, thus continues the trend started with the *Turn of the Cards* album – that of combining unusually beautiful musical qualities (primarily Dunford's melodies and Haslam's voice) with dark subject matter and emotive content, as Renaissance here deals with fear and confusion ('Trip to the Fair'), anger and resentment ('The Vultures Fly High'), and sadness ('Ocean Gypsy').

The next track, and album side, will move in a different direction.

'Song Of Scheherazade' 24:40 (Dunford/Tout/Camp/Thatcher)

Clocking in at almost 25 minutes, and taking up the entire second side of the original LP, 'Song Of Scheherazade', a nine-section suite, is Renaissance's most symphonic piece, and the longest studio track in the band's catalogue.

Contrary to popular belief, and, indeed, to the misinformation contained in the album's original liner notes, it is a new, original composition, and - aside from one repeated six-note motif - not a re-working of Rimsky-Korsakov's famous 1888 symphonic suite, *Scheherazade* (though it is written generally in the style of late romantic Russian music). As Haslam puts it, when it comes to musical adaptations of the story of Scheherazade, 'there are three versions: Ravel, Rimsky-Korsakov, and Renaissance'.

The source material for all of these versions is the initial frame story from *One Thousand and One Nights*, a collection of Middle Eastern folk tales first compiled many centuries ago in Arabic. This frame story concerns an ancient ruler, the Sultan Shahryār, and Scheherazade. When Shahryār learns that his wife has been unfaithful, he has her killed. Knowing that his brother's wife had also been unfaithful, he leaps to the conclusion that all women are this way, and decides to take revenge on the lot of them. His scheme is to marry a succession of virgins, and then to execute each one the next morning, but only (to quote from the spoken introduction to a recording of a live Renaissance performance) after first 'having taken his dastardly pleasure'. After he has killed several brides in this way, his new wife, Scheherazade, embarks on a strategy to save her life. On her wedding night, she tells the Sultan an engrossing story but makes a point of making it last until morning, the time of the scheduled beheading, without completing it. Curious to know how the story ends, Shahryār puts off the execution so that he can hear its conclusion. But that night, when Scheherazade finishes the story, she immediately starts another, leading the Sultan, once again, to postpone the execution, for the same reason. This goes on for 1,001 nights, by which time Shahryār, having fallen in love with Scheherazade, repudiates his murderous plan. While the story seems to be intended as a happy one, in which we can celebrate Scheherazade's brilliant initiative in figuring out how to save her own life, and potentially that of every other young female in the vicinity, one can't help but notice the heavy price she pays – that of having to stay married to a misogynistic serial killer, albeit a reformed one.

The piece opens with a brief section entitled 'Fanfare', composed by Tout, and performed, rather majestically in a stately 4/4 rhythm, by the London Symphony Orchestra's brass players.

It quickly gives way to 'The Betrayal', another instrumental section, this one composed by Camp, Dunford, and Tout. As it begins, the orchestra, with Sullivan's support on drums, plays six leisurely measures in waltz time, before picking up the pace and transitioning back to 4/4. Here the band and orchestra, very successfully merged into one unit, launch into a lively two-minute passage, in which strings, piano, xylophone, and horns take turns in the spotlight, with Camp's bass and Sullivan's drums also prominent in the mix. While this section is quite enjoyable as a piece of music on its own terms, its programmatic value is perhaps more dubious, as the exuberant playing is not particularly suggestive of anything as negative as a 'betrayal'.

The players then quiet down a bit for the beginning of 'The Sultan', a Dunford and Thatcher collaboration, and the first of just three sections of this nine-section suite to feature lyrics. A choir is heard at its outset, singing 'ah's, seemingly from a great distance away, over a repeating Camp bass riff, with occasional interjections from Tout's piano.

When the singing starts we find that it is Camp, taking his first lead vocal since *Prologue*'s 'Kiev', who begins to tell the story of the Sultan and his murderous campaign. Haslam joins him for a couple of lines in each of the first two verses, hitting, and sustaining, a skyscraping G#5 note in each one. The band provides most of the instrumental backing for the first verse, with only occasional contributions from orchestral players. The choir, now seemingly closer to us, and louder in the mix, makes a brief return between the verses.

As the second verse begins, the choir drops out, and the instrumental backing intensifies, with the orchestra playing a more prominent role than it had previously.

Following a brief return of the choir, Haslam and Camp, accompanied by swirling strings and tinkling bell sounds (presumably from a celeste), then sing a new melody as they tell of Scheherazade's brilliant tactic:

> Scheherazade bewitched him
> With songs of jewelled keys
> Princes and of heroes
> And eastern fantasies
> Told him tales of sultans
> And talismans and rings
> A thousand and one nights she sang
> To entertain her king

This leads to an exuberant chorus: 'She sings – Scheherazade, Scheherazade, Scheherazade ...' (with 'Scheherazade' continuing to repeat), as the band (especially Camp, thundering away on bass), orchestra, and choir, all join in on this triumphant passage. The singing eventually yields to a short instrumental interlude, which includes an ascending piano statement that closes out the section on a climactic D# minor chord.

Camp's 'Love Theme', another instrumental section, is next. It starts as a very quiet, classical-sounding, piano piece, by turns atmospheric and melodic. But then the band and orchestra both kick in, providing some dynamic contrast to the section's quiet beginning. Like 'Betrayal', this is successful enough as a stand-alone piece of music, but perhaps less so from a programmatic standpoint, as nothing about it is particularly suggestive of love. As it comes to a close, Tout plays an ascending piano line that is very similar to the one heard at the conclusion of 'The Sultan', but this time terminating in a B minor chord.

The next section, 'The Young Prince And Princess As Told By Scheherazade', a Dunford and Thatcher collaboration, is perhaps the highlight of the entire suite. The band seems to have thought so as well, for when Renaissance has performed in concert just a portion, rather than the entirety, of 'Song of Scheherazade', this is the section they have generally chosen to include as a stand-in for the larger work.

Dunford's acoustic guitar, far less in evidence on the current album than it had been on *Turn Of The Cards*, starts it off. After just a couple of bars of his quiet strumming, Haslam enters to sing, beautifully and highly evocatively, the album's most memorable melody. If one were to choose any one brief musical passage to serve as an example of singing at its loveliest, the first verse that she sings here, accompanied by acoustic guitar, oboe, and, in the latter portion, harp, would not be a bad selection:

And you would cause the sun to see your light and then be shamed
You cover darkness with a thousand secret flames
With your love, oh my love, oh my love, my love
And I would cause the winds to blow a hundred different days
And bring the perfumes of the gardens of the ways
Of your love, oh my love, oh my love, my love

The second verse, sung to a different melody, brings Tout's piano into the proceedings, shortly after which the band and orchestra both kick in, playing with increasing intensity as the verse unfolds, and continuing to do so after Haslam's singing takes a lengthy pause. The section ends with her return to deliver a final line, 'And he would vow to love her for the rest of all his days', as the band and orchestra wind down to a stop.

The next section, 'Festival Preparations', a Camp, Dunford, and Tout collaboration, is another programmatic piece, intended to call to mind images of a happy city joyously preparing for a major public celebration. At first, the playing is so quiet as to be nearly inaudible, as for the better part of a minute we hear the faint stirrings of first one instrument, and then another. As more instruments join in the playing, the track, while still quiet, gradually increases in volume. But the different players make little effort to coordinate their playing at first, giving the section, to this point, a somewhat random quality. My guess is that this represents the city waking up, as the quiet of a sleeping city is gradually replaced by the sound of people, one by one, rising and preparing to start their day. As more and more of them wake up, the playing, while still not very coordinated, gets louder and louder before suddenly, a drum strike, perhaps signalling a call to action, brings the players together to take up a jaunty tune.

The band (piano, bass, and drums) takes this up at first, but the orchestral players and the vocalists (singing 'la la la' vocalise) soon join in, and almost every part of the ensemble – strings, brass, harp, xylophone, woodwinds, singers, and so forth – takes a brief turn in the spotlight. As the tune that they play is a happy one, it easily conjures up, with the help of the section title, images of the city's citizens joyously scurrying about and working together in preparation for a celebratory festival.

When this episode reaches its climax, the section gives way to its calm, quiet coda, in which an oboe conveys a subtle, contemplative melody, as the Renaissance players provide restrained support on celeste, acoustic guitar, bass, drums, and piano.

The next movement, Tout's 'Fugue For The Sultan', a bouncy, baroque-sounding, contrapuntal composition, continues the happy vibe established by 'Festival Preparations'. Tout first establishes its melody on the piano, and then is joined by the orchestra, which further develops and complicates the theme, generating a pleasing complexity through the layering and interweaving of different fragments of, and variations on, the initial piano melody.

Tout's fugue transitions, rather abruptly, to 'The Festival', a Dunford and Thatcher collaboration. It begins with a spirited recapitulation of 'The Betrayal', before the orchestra yields to a quiet acoustic guitar and xylophone passage, which goes on to serve as the foundation for Haslam's lead vocal. She sings, eventually accompanied by other instruments and by one of the band's male singers, a fast-paced song describing the events of the festival – with its food, music, singing, dancing, and crowds of people smiling and laughing as they enjoy a day of festivities in celebration of the Sultan's marriage to Scheherazade.

The section then segues, as the singers render the last syllable of Scheherazade's name, into the 'Finale', which is incompletely credited to Camp, Dunford, and Tout. For some reason, Thatcher's name is omitted, even though her lyrics are sung in this section. Here the band, orchestra, and choir all join in support of Haslam and Camp, as they bring back the final stanza of 'The Sultan', culminating in the repeated, celebratory, singing of Scheherazade's name. The track progresses through these repetitions, getting continuously louder and more intense, and undergoing a key change, before reaching a climax, as Haslam, once again entering the stratosphere, hits, and holds, an A#5 note. The track then slows down, as the orchestra quietly plays a short outro, culminating in a final, sustained, B major chord.

Thus ends the 'Song of Scheherazade', as well as the *Scheherazade and Other Stories* album. Having just produced perhaps their most confident, mature, and consistent album to date, and one that would be almost universally loved by fans and admired by critics, the future for Renaissance looked, at this point, very bright. Little did the band know that the emergence of new musical styles, especially punk and disco, would soon compete for the attention of the listening public, making it more of a challenge for a progressive, classically-inspired, band – the kind that would fill an album side with just one, lengthy, multi-movement suite, and an entire album with just four tracks – to find a sympathetic audience.

Novella (1977)

Personnel:
Jon Camp: bass, vocals, bass pedals, acoustic guitar, cello
Michael Dunford: acoustic guitars (six-string and twelve-string), backing vocals
Annie Haslam: vocals, percussion
Terry Sullivan: drums, percussion, backing vocals, tubular bells, timpani
John Tout: piano, synths, clavinet, percussion, backing vocals
Richard Hewson: orchestral arrangements
Producer: Renaissance and Dick Plant
Release date: March 1977
Highest chart position: 46 (US)
Running time of original LP: 40:12
Note: The 2019 Esoteric label reissue, a 3 CD box set, contains many live recordings among its bonus tracks. These are discussed in a separate chapter devoted to live Renaissance recordings. The box set also includes shortened versions, edited for release as singles, of 'Can You Hear Me?' and 'Midas Man'. These are of little interest.

Despite the declining fortunes of progressive rock as a genre, Renaissance was still flying high in November 1976, as the band took to the studio to record *Novella*. They were coming off a string of four consecutive studio albums, each more successful, both critically and commercially, than its predecessor. And the group's most recent release, a live double album recorded at New York's prestigious Carnegie Hall (discussed in a separate chapter on Renaissance's live recordings), had also won critical acclaim and had sold better than all but one of the band's studio albums – a significant achievement, given the relatively weaker market for live albums. Adding to this momentum was the group's increasing success as a headlining live act, routinely selling out medium-sized concert venues, and playing to wildly appreciative audiences.

With the confidence engendered by this success, Renaissance was able to produce its final masterpiece – another dark, quiet, largely acoustic album, in which every track is a winner. There would be excellent tracks on many future Renaissance albums and some good ones on all of them, but here, for the fifth consecutive time, the band was able to put together an album that sparkles with greatness from start to finish – the last time it would be able to accomplish that difficult and impressive feat.

'Can You Hear Me?' 13:39 (Camp/Dunford/Thatcher)

The album opener is another classic Renaissance epic, with a running time of over thirteen minutes. Continuing the band's tradition of dealing primarily with dark subject matter, this one is about the harmful effects of social isolation in the city. It describes lonely people who, despite being surrounded by crowds, fail to connect with others, or even to notice them on a personal level. The metaphor that Thatcher uses in the song's lyrics is that of hearing, where recognising another as a unique individual, caring about his or her concerns, and sharing something of oneself with that person, is a matter of hearing the person's 'call', picking it out from the unending din of city life, and the undifferentiated anonymity of individuals lost in big city crowds. Haslam's stellar lead vocal, in which she sings from the perspective of one who is suffering from social isolation, brings out all of the pathos of such a condition, as she repeatedly, and with increasing desperation, sings the lines 'Can you hear me?', 'Can you hear me call?', and 'Can you hear me call your name?'

Musically, one of the most notable features of the track is its unusual approach to dynamics. As one might expect of such a lengthy piece, there is plenty of dynamic variation in the form of contrasting soft and loud passages. But what is surprising is the fact that most of the track is relatively quiet, with the louder episodes being both few in number and short in duration. One would have thought, given the song's lyrical content, that the arrangement would attempt to replicate the noisiness of city life, which the lyrics explicitly cite as one of the hardships of city life, and one of the causes of social disconnection:

Night time people find it hard
To hear themselves above the noise....

Put it down to city nights
Oh if I understood
Passing by so far from me
I'd reach you if I could
Can you hear me?
Can you hear me?

I'd guess the band went in the opposite direction as loudness in music often communicates excitement and intensity, whereas the feeling of loneliness the band wanted to convey is better expressed through quiet sounds.

One particular use of dynamic contrast is worthy of mention in this context. At about three minutes into the track (following a very melodic introduction, in which the band and orchestra, once again, completely merge so as to play together as a single unit), Dunford can be heard playing a repeating lick on his acoustic twelve-string guitar. Shortly thereafter Haslam enters to deliver the song's opening lyrics, accompanied, at first, only by Dunford's guitar. But as more instruments gradually join the mix, we eventually lose sight of Dunford's quiet picking. However, at several points during the song Haslam pauses her singing, and the other instrumentalists also either pause or play quietly, and suddenly we notice the subtle presence of Dunford's guitar, playing the same lick it had played previously (or a variation on it, as sometimes he stays on an E minor chord, while other times he alternates between E minor and A major) – thus creating the impression (a false one, but that doesn't matter for the point I'm making) that it had been there all along, but that we simply hadn't noticed it, because it had been drowned out by louder sounds. This is a nice musical parallel to the idea of persons, in their distinctive individuality, being missed amongst the 'noise' (both literal, in terms of auditory noise, and metaphorical, in terms of an excess of activity, of things going on, of 'hustle and bustle') of city life. Although this interpretation may sound far fetched as it is described here on the page, in my experience, it hits one hard when actually listening to the track, as one is repeatedly caught off guard by the seemingly magical reappearance of Dunford's quiet little guitar lick.

As mentioned, following the first iteration of that lick Haslam sings the first verse, and it immediately communicates the song's central concern:

> Morning people take the news
> A paper window on a world
> They live on undisturbed
> Thoughts may fly like lonely birds
> And lost behind the silent words
> Voices are unheard
> Put it down to city life
> Oh if I understood
> Passing by so easily
> I'd reach you if I could
> Can you hear me?
> Can you hear me?

Transitioning from one catchy, memorable, melody to another, she then sings the chorus, which ends with these lines: 'Some city flights leave in the morning/ Some city nights end without warning/ Can you hear me call?' And what is it that we hear, immediately after Haslam inquires as to what we can hear? The answer is – Dunford's lonely little guitar lick.

The next thing we hear is the second verse, which, with the 'morning people' having already been dealt with, concerns itself instead with the evening people:

> Evening people see the day
> A silhouette on every face
> A shadow on their eyes
> I take my place within the crowd
> We walk the dusty streets around
> Encompassing our lives
> Put it down to city times
> Oh if I understood
> Passing by so casually
> I'd reach you if I could
> Can you hear me?
> Can you hear me?

The instrumental backing for this second verse is much thicker than it had been for the first verse, with Sullivan's surprising glockenspiel leading the way.

The second verse, like the first, is followed by a rendition of the chorus, which this time ends, not with one insistent 'Can you hear me call?' query, but rather three, with the first two immediately answered by the return of Dunford's lick.

The final iteration of Haslam's question brings about a key change, and a lengthy, but noticeably quiet, instrumental section. Tout starts it off with a solo on one of his keyboards. Its soft, faraway, quality is thrown into sharp relief when it is briefly joined by Camp's bass and Sullivan's drums, which, by contrast, sound very present. The playing is then abruptly terminated by the arrival of a gong strike. As the gong strike's decay eventually allows other sounds to be heard, the only one that emerges is Dunford's acoustic twelve-string, continuing with its signature lick.

Eventually, a very quiet, extremely distant-sounding keyboard can be heard, creating a soft background over which Camp proceeds to play an extraordinarily quiet and delicate bass solo, using effect pedals to give his bass a muted, and far away, sound. Sullivan provides support in the form of a light and subtle glockenspiel part, further contributing to the diaphanous feel of this passage. Tout then joins in to play the melody of the chorus on an electronic keyboard, probably a synthesizer. Like the other players, his contribution is extremely quiet and sounds as if it were being played several city blocks away from us.

At one point the quiet is interrupted by the loud return of a brief drum and vocalise blast that had first been heard during the track's instrumental introduction. But when the blast dies down, the quiet passage returns, as we hear, in every case faintly, and with a drifting, faraway quality: an electronic keyboard drone, Dunford's twelve-string lick, Sullivan's twinkly glockenspiel, Camp's muted, pedals-altered, bass, occasional cymbal strikes, and, eventually, a return of Tout's synthesizer re-statement of the chorus – all without generating even half as much noise as one would need to wake the lightest of sleepers.

A bit later, a second break in this quiet occurs with a return of the brief drum and vocalise bit that had provided the first such break. But the eventual decay of this blast reveals, once again, Dunford's recurring guitar lick, which goes on to serve, this time, as the accompaniment to a new vocal section, with yet another catchy and memorable melody, different from those of the verses and chorus. Ironically, given the quietness of the preceding lengthy instrumental section, Haslam here sings of being drowned out by noise, and of that being a barrier to communication:

Calling to the sky
The thunder drowns my voice within the rain
And I know you're near me

And I call throughout the storm
I know that you don't hear me
I call your name
I call your name
I call your name

This is a high part, as Haslam reaches an F#5 note at its highest point. Often when signing in that range, she powerfully blasts the notes, as if to demonstrate her ability to move about comfortably there. But in this passage, without actually straining, she employs a more modest singing style, in which she communicates the idea that she is reaching, somewhat uncomfortably, for the high notes, analogous to reaching out to another person, in a desperate attempt at meaningful interpersonal communication – an effect that is underscored by the fact that the highest note in her singing coincides with the word 'you're'. Then, when she repeatedly sings, 'I call your name', she does so softly, and with (I assume, deliberately), a thinner, less full and rounded, vocal tone than she normally achieves, effectively communicating the enervating sadness of a lonely person deprived of desired human contact.

But then, a high-energy Sullivan drum fill kicks the track into high gear, as the band, now playing with energy, and at high volume, supports the singers, with Haslam in the lead, as they sing, and then repeat, a gloriously triumphant melismatic fragment in 'ah' vocalise. This gives way to Haslam, now singing powerfully, confidently, and in a rich, rounded tone, with support from the orchestra's strings and blaring brass, as she renders the lines, 'Can you hear me call your name?/ Can you hear me call?/ Hear me call your name'. However, as the orchestral blasts die down, and the softer, subtler instrumentation returns, Haslam also switches back to a thinner, more vulnerable sounding, voice, as she plaintively sings, 'I call your name/ I call your name/ Can you hear me call your name?', beautifully conveying her sorrowful disappointment at the lack of response to her calls and her desperation in continuing to issue them.

The orchestra, as if rallying to her support, then begins to establish a lively, tuneful, high energy, background part, quickly to be joined by the band, as strings, bass, xylophone, and drums all compete for the spotlight. When Haslam then returns to deliver the next (and final) verse, she, too, as if heartened by the friendly efforts of the instrumentalists, sings with renewed confidence and power, even as she continues to sing of social isolation in the city, and does so with lyrics that are just as pessimistic as those of the previous verses.

The final verse leads to the final chorus, which ends, as if to underscore the fact that no solution to the problem that was identified at the outset of the song is now being offered at its conclusion, with Haslam three times powerfully demanding, on top of forceful orchestral accompaniment, 'Can you hear me call'?

Following the final iteration of this question, the players strike a final chord and allow it to fade toward silence, thus signalling the end of the track. This terminal silence is never reached, however, as the track instead simply segues into the next one, with the final chord of 'Can You Hear Me?', after it has faded down almost to total silence, continuing on to function also as the very quiet first chord of the next song, 'The Sisters'.

'The Sisters' 7:14 (Dunford/Thatcher/Tout)

A minor key ballad, this one features a melancholic melody that fits its subject matter. It is a tale of despairing missionaries struggling sorrowfully to keep their faith as they confront the daily suffering of the poor labourers who they try to help.

Thatcher's lyrics are a meditation on the ancient theological 'problem of evil'. The problem, for believers in an infinitely powerful and infinitely good God, is one of reconciling these traits with the palpable presence of evil in the form of suffering (especially, though the song doesn't go in this direction, the unmerited suffering of the obviously innocent, such as animals or very young children). The problem is that an infinitely good God would be infinitely opposed to evil, and thus infinitely dedicated to eradicating it and replacing it with good. And an infinitely powerful God, that is, one with infinite ability, would be able to eliminate evil. But if God is both powerful enough to rid the world of evil and good enough to want this result, then why is there evil? Why, specifically, is there so much suffering?

The lyrics, conveyed beautifully, and very sensitively, by Haslam, tell, in the past tense, of 'sisters' who worked hard, and with great dedication, to help the poor, for example, by baking bread for them to eat. But alas, though 'they cared and tried', they were 'worn with their fears and the years of heartbreak'. The men they tried to help, labourers, stained by dust and sweat from working for 'days in the angry sun', 'were weak, and they cried', as they asked, 'Sisters, make us holy'.

In response,

The sisters prayed, 'Give us hope for something'.
The men asked, 'Where is your God today?'
And the empty eyes as the sisters prayed
Held their thoughts unspoken

There was nothing they could do
Earth was dust for miles around
Nothing new survived

The climax of the song arrives with the next lines: 'Everything was barren on the land/ And the truth they tried to understand/ Just died'. These are the only lines in the song to be repeated, as they are resurrected, by themselves, unconnected to the verse in which they had originally appeared, at the end of the song, following a substantial instrumental passage that otherwise takes up the final three minutes or more of the track. Moreover, the highest note that Haslam hits is to be found here, on both instances in which she sings the word 'died'.

With regard to the arrangement, a few points are noteworthy. This is the first Renaissance track not to begin with silence. Rather, as already noted, 'Can You Hear Me?' segues into it. It is also an orchestrated piece, and, as has become a Renaissance trademark, the integration of band and orchestra is perfect, as the orchestra's strings and horns complement the band's guitars, keyboards, and drums, with no sense that two different groups of players are being awkwardly thrown together.

Perhaps the main instrumental highlight of the piece is the use of classical, nylon-string, guitar, which is heard, first in a support capacity, and then as the featured instrument, taking a long, and very enjoyable, solo in the middle of the track. The style of the solo is Spanish, bordering on flamenco, and sounds nothing like anything that Dunford had played on previous Renaissance recordings. While it is certainly possible, for all I know, that he is capable of such playing, and simply had not had occasion to show this previously, it is noteworthy that Camp, who had not received an acoustic guitar credit on either of the two previous albums, gets one here, so it may be that he is the player.

In any case, the other musical highlight that I will mention is the lovely, minor-key, choir-like, wordless vocalising that is heard in a passage starting at 0:57. This passage, which is somewhat reminiscent of the similarly evocative choir-like singing on 'Golden Thread', a song by the original incarnation of Renaissance, on the *Illusion* album, communicates the sad hopelessness of the sisters as least as powerfully as Thatcher's lyrics and Haslam's lead vocal performance do. A different choir-like vocalise passage, this time with the parts staggered, is almost equally effective. It can be heard just before, and then during the tail end of, the classical guitar solo.

'Midas Man' 5:45 (Dunford/Thatcher)

Continuing the dark tone of the album, 'Midas Man' deals with the endless suffering caused by greed. According to the ancient legend, King Midas was a man who, having been granted one wish by the god Dionysus, chose to be granted a 'golden touch', wherein anything he touched would turn to gold. At first, he was delighted by this gift, as he saw that he could effortlessly multiply his wealth simply by touching inexpensive items in his possession, thereby instantly transforming them into valuable gold pieces. However, he realised his horrible mistake when he discovered that food and drink also turned into inedible gold the moment he touched it – a parable making the obvious, but apparently necessary, point that financial wealth is not the only thing of value and that the excessive pursuit of it, to the neglect of these other values, is ruinous.

Thatcher's lyrics, presumably about our modern King Midases, rather than the king of ancient legend, also bring out the social costs of greed – the way in which an excessive love of money, in addition to being self-destructive, leads the greedy person to trample over others in its pursuit:

> I'll take from the blind and I'll get up ahead
> I'll sneak up behind and I'll steal
> I'll take all that you have
> And then all that you've concealed
> I'll take anything I can get
> I'll make you, I'll break you, and I'll make you sweat
> Nothing is worth nothing unless it's
> Made for Midas Man

Musically, like every Dunford composition to this point, it has a very catchy vocal melody (both verses and chorus). Haslam takes advantage of a rare opportunity to sing in her lower register, going all the way down to F#3 in another flawless vocal performance.

The arrangement is somewhat unusual for Renaissance. It is dominated by acoustic guitars, but here played in a heavy, highly rhythmic, style, and apparently massed, through multi-tracking, so as to achieve a thick sound, far removed from the lighter effects we usually get from Dunford. Sullivan mostly avoids his drum kit, and instead, in a delightfully inventive move, so very appropriate to the song's subject matter, provides percussive support by shaking a bag filled with coins! And he brings drama to both iterations of the chorus by adding the bold sound of tubular bells.

Another interesting feature of the arrangement is the use of an F# pedal in the verses, which stays put while the chords above it change. That stability from the fixed pedal makes the harmonic motion behind it sound stealthy, like Midas himself, sneaking up behind you to steal what you have. Similarly, the creepiest lines in the song, 'sell my soul', and, later, 'sell your soul', are set to an appropriately creepy diminished triad melody.

A final noteworthy passage occurs towards the end, wherein Haslam sings a descending melodic fragment to the words 'Midas, Midas, Midas, Midas man', as Camp, echoing moves he had made twice previously, sings a part which, through non-alignment, seems to swim over, under, and in between her sequence – a lovely moment in another darkly pretty song.

'The Captive Heart' 4:12 (Camp/Dunford)

The first of two Camp and Dunford collaborations on the album (which are also the first two in the Renaissance catalogue), this bittersweet ballad is about repeatedly failing at love, but nonetheless persevering and trying again.

The arrangement is highly unusual for Renaissance, in that it features only piano and vocals. The classical influence is clearly evident in Tout's elegant, lengthy (about 50 seconds), baroque sounding introduction. He also provides the sole instrumental accompaniment to the vocals and plays a short outro at the end.

The vocal arrangement is one of the most varied in the Renaissance catalogue. Haslam sings all but one line of each of the first two verses alone. Camp sings the last line of those verses ('Finding out the hard way') alone, harmonising with himself through overdubbing. Haslam and Camp sing the third verse, which is really a half-verse, together in unison, separated by an octave. Haslam sings the first chorus alone, harmonising with herself by means of a high, trilling, overdubbed part. And the vocal highlight is the second chorus, which is arranged similarly to the first, except that this time the two Haslams are placed out of alignment with one another, thus creating counterpoint.

The tone of Camp's lyrics, very well matched by the melody, is more that of wistfulness than full-blown sorrow, as it deals with struggle and disappointment, rather than absolute failure and despondency. The final half-verse represents the song's mood well: 'No easy path to conquer/ Trying to compromise/ Climbing through my anguish/ I see your fading eyes', as does the final line of the chorus: 'Loving takes a life of trying, so it seems'.

Though it is the shortest and slightest track on the album, 'The Captive Heart' is full of subtle pleasures, and an enjoyable listen, from start to finish.

'Touching Once (Is So Hard To Keep)' 9:22 (Camp/Dunford)

This proggy classic keeps alive Renaissance's perfect seven-album streak of closing out each album with an epic work of at least nine minutes in length.

It has an unusual structure. Renaissance tracks of this length usually alternate vocal and instrumental sections. Here, however, the song's many instrumental twists and turns are concentrated together in one continuous sequence in the middle. Running to well over five minutes, this band and orchestra workout is framed by the more conventional verse/chorus sections that precede it, and the modified chorus that succeeds it.

The track begins with a brief, loud blast from the band and orchestra, playing (as usual) as a well-coordinated, well-integrated unit. This gives way to another short passage, a quiet Tout piano solo, in which he introduces the melody of the first verse, which Haslam then proceeds to sing. Like almost all of the other vocal melodies on the first five albums of the Haslam era, this is a shapely and memorable one, well conveyed by Haslam's strong voice.

Her accompaniment here, consistent with the band's practice on many other tracks, is gradually layered in, as she is supported first by Tout's piano alone, with Dunford's acoustic guitar and Camp's bass subsequently joining in, followed by Sullivan's drums .

The meaning of the lyrics that she sings, written by Camp, rather than Thatcher, is not obvious, at least to me. My best guess is that the song is at least partially about political refugees, fleeing oppression and embarking on a difficult journey toward a new home. These lines, the first ones that Haslam sings, are the ones that create that impression:

Leaving all their thoughts behind
Passing over timeless wastes of ecstasy
Freedom strangled at the source
Takes the only charted course
That leads them home

The first verse leads, without a break, directly to the first chorus. Haslam sings its first couple of lines alone, before Camp joins her for its remainder, doubling her an octave lower. The third voice in the mix is Haslam's own, singing an overdubbed harmony part.

As she then transitions to the second verse, the layering in of instrumental accompaniment continues, with orchestral instruments gradually joining in, leading, eventually, to a full, complex, mix. As before, the verse is followed immediately by the second chorus, with Camp reviving his vocal part in the same manner. The words to the second chorus differ from those of the first, and I find their meaning unclear – a point that, as mentioned, generally holds for this song's lyrics. These words, which Haslam and Camp sing in the second chorus, are representative of those in the song as a whole (the last four of these lines are repeated, just before the track ends):

A part of what is held inside, a deep regret
Taking over all that a heart's request
Answered by cries from a wilderness
Found forgotten lying in deeper sleep
Touching once is so hard to keep

In any case, at the conclusion of the singing of the just-quoted lyrics, the song's long instrumental section begins, starting with a sudden, loud, staccato, five-note pattern, played four times in succession. This leads to a delightfully melodic passage, in which a four-chord progression is first established, at a fast tempo, over which the band's singers then sing a 'la la la' vocalise pattern, with their non-aligned voices overlapping one another, in an enchanting counterpoint. After they have gone through this pattern twice, the drums and chord-playing instruments drop out, leaving behind only a minimal level of instrumental accompaniment, the better to spotlight the continuing 'la la la' singing. At the conclusion of this episode, a short orchestral passage brings about a return of the descending staccato pattern, this time conveyed vocally, in multi-singer vocalise, and with the pattern extended to nine notes in two of its iterations.

This leads to a quiet, far away sounding passage, in which Dunford's acoustic guitar picks out a background pattern, over which a solo is played by what initially sounds like an oboe, but ends up (as it gets into its higher register) sounding more like an electronic keyboard. Tout's piano eventually takes over the melody, as Camp's bass moves higher in the mix.

Tout then gives way to Dunford, who plays a lovely arpeggiated chord progression on his twelve-string acoustic guitar. When he switches to strumming, this inaugurates a tempo shift, as Camp takes up the melody that had been implied by Dunford's chord sequence, playing it on his now effects-laden bass. The orchestra comes in shortly thereafter, before yielding to Sullivan for a drum fill, after which the orchestra immediately returns.

At first the low-pitched strings take the melody over from Camp, who continues to sizzle, though now in a supporting role. The horns, very low in the mix at first, then begin to state the melody at a higher pitch, and with a different rhythm. As the strings continue to play the melody in long-held notes, changing notes only when the underlying chord changes, the horns now play an insistent rhythmic pattern. As the horns are getting louder, a saxophone enters, at first heard only faintly, as it plays occasional melodic fragments, somewhat in the manner of an improvised solo over the chord progression, but so low in the mix as not to be immediately perceived as such. Soon the higher-pitched strings join in, and the track is now really cooking, with Camp still thundering away on bass, Sullivan having a bash on drums, the orchestral strings and brass fully engaged, and the saxophone starting to move up in the mix.

Seven and a half minutes in, the sax solo, by an uncredited member of the orchestra, takes off in earnest, adding a jazzy feel to the proceedings. As it does so, wordless background 'ah's become audible, adding another layer, and further intensity, to the mix. The excitement only increases as the wordless vocals become progressively louder, thus competing with the strings and the saxophone for the spotlight, with Camp and Sullivan refusing to cede ground in the process.

This episode reaches its climax after eight minutes, at which time the players begin a transition to the final vocal section. It is sung by Haslam alone this time, without Camp, at a slower tempo, and with much louder and more involved instrumental backing.

The final line that she sings is the title of the song, 'Touching once is so hard to keep'. As she reaches the word 'hard', Camp reprises the descending five-note staccato pattern on his bass. Shortly joined by the orchestra, he plays it a total of nine times as Haslam completes her vocal, going up to a D5 note on the final word, 'keep'. As she holds the note, the orchestra immediately goes back for a tenth iteration of the descending staccato sequence, but then, as if suddenly noticing that Haslam had stopped singing, abruptly stops after four notes, thus bringing the track, and the *Novella* album, to a sudden end on an unlikely B note.

Though now definitely swimming against the tide of popular and critical taste, Renaissance had succeeded in making an excellent album on their own terms – a progressive album, containing two very lengthy tracks (as usual, too long for radio), and (yet again) a dark album, dealing with loneliness and social disconnection in the city, human suffering and the loss of religious faith that it engenders, the cruelty and personal and social destructiveness of greed, the difficulty of finding and sustaining love, and (possibly) political repression and the plight of refugees. In spite of its unfashionable style and subject matter, the album was well-received, and found an audience, at least in the United States, bringing the band its highest chart placement to date. Even greater commercial success, though arguably at the expense of artistic decline, lay in the near future.

A Song For All Seasons (1978)

Personnel:
Jon Camp: bass, vocals, bass pedals, electric guitar
Michael Dunford: electric and six- and twelve-string acoustic guitars
Annie Haslam: vocals
Terry Sullivan: drums, percussion
John Tout: keyboards
Louis Clark: orchestral arrangements
Harry Rabinowitz: orchestra conductor, orchestral arrangement on 'She is Love'
The Royal Philharmonic Orchestra
Producer: David Hentschel
Release date: March 1978
Highest chart position: 35 (UK), 58 (US)
Running time of original LP: 44:36
Note: The 2019 Esoteric label reissue, a 3 CD box set, contains among its bonus tracks many live concert recordings, as well as recordings made for BBC Radio and for the Top of the Pops television program. These are discussed in a separate chapter devoted to live Renaissance recordings. The box set also includes the promotional single edit of 'Northern Lights', which is of little interest.

When Renaissance entered the studio in November 1977 to begin work on the sixth studio album of the Haslam era, one might have expected them to stick to the progressive/symphonic style they had employed on the previous five. After all, each of those, including their latest, *Novella*, had outsold its predecessor, received critical acclaim, and generated increased ticket sales for the band's concerts.

But on the other hand, Renaissance albums were only charting in the US, and specifically not in the band's home, the UK. Moreover, such chart success as the band was achieving had been entirely on the album side, as they had never been able to crack the singles market on either side of the Atlantic. And popular music fashions were changing, with punk, 'new wave', and disco clearly on the rise, and progressive rock, just as clearly, on the decline. Perhaps because of a perceived need to change in order to remain viable, or, to put a less pessimistic spin on it, perhaps because of a perceived opportunity to take a step forward by making concessions to the newer styles (maybe thereby making a breakthrough in the UK and on the singles charts), the band took a different course for its new album, *A Song for all Seasons*.

One significant change is the return of the electric guitar, which had been absent from the previous three studio albums. Here, played by both Dunford and Camp, it gives the band's sound a harder edge, and more of a mainstream rock sound, less suggestive of classical music. Similarly, Tout makes far less use than he had on previous albums of piano, and far more use, in keeping with contemporary trends, of synthesizers.

Even more importantly, the band starts to move away from its penchant for lengthy pieces – heretofore a defining characteristic of the Renaissance style. Whereas on the preceding five studio albums only eight of 27 tracks (fewer than one in three) had clocked in at a running time of fewer than five minutes, by contrast, fully six of the eight tracks on *A Song for all Seasons* come in under that time limit. The radical nature of this departure is made more manifest by the fact that only two of the ten tracks on the first two Renaissance albums (those from the pre-Haslam era), were of such brevity, and only one of eight on the sole live album released by the Haslam-era band to date.

From a purely commercial standpoint, this strategy of moving toward a more straight-ahead rock style, with (for the most part) briefer, less complex, song structures, turned out to be a success, at least in the short term. The band was able to score its first hit single, and a major one at that, as 'Northern Lights' cracked the top ten in England, resulting in the band receiving an invitation to perform on the popular British television show, *Top of the Pops*. And while the album charted in the US, of greater significance is the fact that the band was finally able to place an album in the charts in the UK, the first time it had done so since the very first Renaissance album, way back in 1969, but here reaching a higher chart position, at 35.

Although Renaissance had largely been spared the harsh criticism that had been directed at other progressive rock bands, one can wonder whether the group's change in direction might also have been partially in response to such criticism as they had received. The criticisms mainly fell into three categories. First, the music of Renaissance, with its 'soft' instrumentation (acoustic guitar, piano, and frequently strings), its classical influences, its lovely melodies, and Haslam's gorgeous voice, was simply too pretty, too beautiful, too melodic – with not enough grit, not enough power, not enough astringency, not enough rock. Secondly, the band kept doing the same thing over and over again (long, melodic, multi-section, classically-influenced pieces), with not enough stylistic variation. Finally, long, serious, classically-influenced songs are, in a rock context, 'pretentious' and 'pompous'. (This last one is the generic criticism routinely thrown in the faces of all of the progressive rock bands. Haslam's response: 'I've seen reviews. How can you call Yes pompous? They're flipping amazing. It's a silly word. I don't get it'.) Notice that the band's new direction – a harder-edged, more rock-oriented sound, incorporating electric guitar and synthesizers, with fewer (only two) of the 'pretentious', out-of-date, proggy pieces, and many more that are in keeping with current fashions – addresses every one of these complaints.

On the positive side, the two lengthy progressive-rock tracks, the ones that are most consistent with Renaissance's established style, are both outstanding, and 'Northern Lights', the band's breakthrough hit single, is indeed a superior pop song, fully meriting its commercial success. Moreover, there are nice moments on most of the other tracks as well, making the album, on the whole, a good one.

But two problems are starting to emerge here. Although Renaissance had been given a genre classification as a 'progressive rock' or 'symphonic rock' band, its style, up to now, had really been unique. No other band had sounded remotely like Renaissance. Here, however, for the first time, there are many moments in which the group's sound has a generic quality, readily distinguishable from other bands only by the unique timbre of Haslam's voice. Secondly, one of the group's biggest strengths had been the almost uniformly superior quality of its melodies, with its lengthy tracks typically packed with shapely, catchy, memorable tunes, distributed all throughout the pieces – verses, choruses, middle eights, intros, outros, instrumental breaks, 'la la la' vocalise sections, and so forth – and its shorter songs, such as 'Carpet of the Sun' or 'The Vultures Fly High', also exhibiting an attractively tuneful quality, from start to finish. But here, the quality of the melodies is less consistent. The album does contain some outstanding ones – more than one finds on most rock albums. But others are merely serviceable – a criticism that would not have been applicable to any of the albums in the *Prologue* to *Novella* sequence.

'Opening Out' 4:15 (Camp/Dunford)

The album opener is a bit of a mixed bag. On the positive side, the production is stellar, and the arrangement, which features a richly complex interplay among the band and orchestral instruments, is equally impressive. The vocal melody is good, and really shines early in the track, enhanced, as is typically the case, by the quality of Haslam's lead vocal.

But on the negative side, from a structural standpoint, the track sounds unfinished, more like an introduction to a larger section that never arrives than a completed, self-contained, piece of music. Several factors conspire to create that impression.

First, Haslam's vocal is preceded by a substantial instrumental introduction. Generally, introductory music (and this does, indeed, sound introductory) sets the stage for the much more substantial main body of the track, to follow. In the case of Renaissance, an introductory instrumental section lasting well over a minute would tend to indicate a much longer piece, but this song contains only a few vocal sections from Haslam, interspersed with some lengthy instrumental passages. At the end of the song, she sings a grand total of two lines, and then, utterly without warning, abruptly stops, mid-verse, with the track ending in a fade-out just a few seconds later. This ending sounds forced, arbitrary, and pointless.

Finally, and perhaps most significantly, some of the track's musical themes are taken up again in the next piece, 'Day of the Dreamer'. One might hazard a guess that this lead-off track is intended as a kind of overture to the album, as its title, 'Opening Out', might suggest. But an overture typically introduces themes heard throughout the larger work, and that is clearly not the case here. Thus, one is left with the impression that 'Opening Out' may have begun life as a part of 'Day of the Dreamer', only to be excised from it, and transformed, at least nominally, into a stand-alone piece, perhaps to avoid having one of the album's key tracks run to a length of fourteen minutes or more.

'Day Of The Dreamer' 9:43 (Camp/Dunford)

The first of its two proggy epics, this complex, multi-section piece is one of the album's highlights.

It starts off with a brief orchestral blast, before giving way to a quiet introductory passage on Tout's piano. Then the bass and drums kick in, signalling a transition to Haslam's rendition of the first verse. The backing instrumentation is fairly dense, as it involves both the band and orchestra and builds in intensity as Haslam completes the first verse and moves on to the chorus, on which she is joined by Camp.

The shift from verse to chorus brings with it a shift in time signature, as the straight-ahead 4/4 rhythm of the verse gives way to the more complex meter of the chorus.

Following the completion of the second chorus, the band and orchestra join forces for a dazzling three-minute instrumental section, full of shifts in tempo, instrumentation, and mood, including, a quotation of a melodic fragment from 'Opening Out'.

At just before the six-minute mark, Haslam returns to sing, very tenderly, a new melody, different from that of the verses or chorus. At the conclusion of this vocal section, the orchestra takes over its melody, carried first by horns, and then by strings, before taking up an energetic, rhythmic, ascending theme that ushers in a reiteration of the chorus.

Its conclusion, in turn, yields to a restatement of a riff borrowed from 'Opening Out'. Here it is played four times, with the intensity increasing with each repetition, as more and more instruments (including electric guitar) join in, and as other instruments achieve higher and higher pitch and/or volume levels. The track then reaches its climax, as the orchestra briefly, and very loudly, recapitulates a fragment of the song's vocal melody, before ending, majestically, on an A major chord.

'Closer Than Yesterday' 3:19 (Camp/Dunford)

This short song, in radical contrast to its immediate predecessor, features a very simple structure: two verses and two choruses, framed by a very brief instrumental intro and outro. Moreover, the instrumentation here – again, completely unlike 'Day of the Dreamer' – is quite sparse, with neither drums nor the orchestra in evidence, and Camp's bass making just two brief appearances.

The track begins with a flute-sounding keyboard playing a short melodic fragment over a background of Dunford's finger-picked acoustic guitar. At fifteen seconds in, Dunford switches to a steady, rhythmic, strumming pattern, over which Haslam immediately enters to sing the first verse. For most of this verse, he alone accompanies her, and even as other instruments eventually join in (bass for the last part of each verse, a tambourine on the choruses and toward the end of the second verse, and understated, background electronic keyboards throughout the latter part of the track), his steady strumming remains the rhythmic backbone of the piece. At the conclusion of the second verse, Tout and Dunford return to play an outro – a variation, of about the same duration, of the fragment they had first played as an intro.

By far the best part of the piece – the one without which it would be nothing more than a moderately pretty, but otherwise quite ordinary, track – is the chorus, in which Haslam, through overdubbing, harmonises with herself, as her non-aligned voices interweave in a manner similar to that of 'The Captive Heart' on the previous album.

'Kindness (At The End)' 4:48 (Camp)

This song, both written and sung by Camp, stands as an example of his increasing involvement in determining the band's direction. Having received no songwriting credits on any of the first three albums on which he played (though he claims to have composed some sections, uncredited), he finally received a credit on *Scheherazade And Other Stories*, followed by three on *Novella*, and now an astonishing six (out of eight total tracks) on *A Song For All Seasons*, with 'Kindness (At the End)' being the one song he is credited as having written alone, with no collaborator. His role as a lyricist, in particular, is at this point expanding dramatically, as he, with Thatcher's declining involvement, apparently wrote the lyrics to five songs on the current album, having contributed in that way to just two tracks on the immediately preceding album, and to none at all prior to that. Much the same can be said about his role as a lead vocalist. Here he takes the lead on two tracks, after having sung, aside from a section of 'Song Of Scheherazade', only one lead vocal on any of the first five albums on which he appeared (on 'Kiev', from the very first album, *Prologue*).

The structure of this one, like 'Opening Out', is an anomaly in the Renaissance catalogue, in that its extensive instrumental introduction (one minute, forty seconds in duration), leads one to expect a lengthy, multi-section track, only to find that Camp, at the conclusion of the introduction, simply sings the song straight through without a break (two verses, chorus, one more verse, final chorus), bringing the piece home in under five minutes. The lyrics (which appear to be about the end of a relationship), the vocal melodies, and Camp's lead vocal, are all thoroughly competent, professional, and modestly enjoyable – but they fail to catch fire, or stand out as exceptional.

The instrumental introduction is more interesting. It begins with Tout, playing a mournful melody on organ. When Sullivan's drums, and then Camp's thundering bass, kick in a few seconds later, the trio could easily be mistaken for Emerson, Lake & Palmer – and the excitement generated by their high-energy groove only increases at about 0:36, as an electric guitar line joins in the mix.

This fun, rocking passage gives way to an arpeggiated keyboard riff, which, after being joined by some finger-picking acoustic guitar, serves as the foundation over which Camp sings the first verse.

While Camp then proceeds, as mentioned, to sing the verses and choruses straight through from start to finish, he and the band attempt to maintain interest by varying the accompaniment to his singing. For the second verse, the arpeggiated keyboard pattern drops out, as a classical guitar takes its place as the main supporting instrument. The entire band then joins in for the chorus and continues to provide rock-band style accompaniment for the third verse and final chorus, with further variation now coming from the backing vocal arrangement – with Camp harmonising with himself through multi-tracking on the choruses, and doing so with his voices non-aligned, creating counterpoint, on the third verse.

At the completion of the singing, the track goes out the way it came in, with a fifteen-second organ solo by Tout, reprising his opening riff, but now in a minor key.

'Back Home Once Again' 3:16 (Camp/Dunford)

This track began life as a commissioned piece. The band's original recording of it was used as the opening theme for the English television series *The Paper Lads*, an award-winning children's show, broadcast nationally from 1977 to 1979, dealing with the adventures of a group of children as they carried out their newspaper delivery jobs. The track that appears on the album is a longer, re-recorded version of this happy, poppy, song.

Haslam sounds great singing the verses, but the track really comes alive on the extremely catchy chorus, on which she harmonises with herself through multi-tracking.

Though the original recording apparently has not been officially released, it can be found on YouTube, and it is instructive to compare it to the later, album version. The just-mentioned use of multi-tracking is absent from the original version, and its addition is one respect in which the re-make stands as an improvement. As the chorus is the best part of the song, a second advantage of the album version is that in it we hear the chorus twice (and with different lyrics each time), whereas in the original version we get the chorus only once.

In other respects, however, one might well prefer the earlier recording. The re-make has a busier arrangement, and a louder, thicker sound, with more instruments involved, and this, arguably, does not suit the piece well. Moreover, much of the increased length of the album version comes from the almost one-minute long instrumental coda that adds little of interest.

'She Is Love' 4:13 (Dunford/Thatcher)

The second of two Camp lead vocals on the album, this almost unlistenable track is one of the few genuine disasters in the Renaissance catalogue. Haslam, who otherwise sings the praises of this album, is on record as not liking this particular recording. And Camp bluntly states, 'I hate that song!'

The instrumental backing is unusual for Renaissance – just the orchestra, plus a bit of Tout's piano. The vocal melody, insofar as one can detect it from

Camp's strained and effects-laden vocal, is subtle at best, unmelodic at worst. So what we have here is a track in which a singer struggles in a valiant effort to carry a weak tune that is, in his own words, 'completely out of my range', against an unpleasantly thick and syrupy orchestral background.

How did this happen? Here accounts differ. Camp's recollection is that the orchestral accompaniment was recorded first, with the vocal to be added later. Then, when Haslam attempted to record the vocal, her several attempts left her dissatisfied, thus leaving the job to the unfortunate Camp, who was, by his own admission, not equal to the challenge, despite his best efforts. Haslam's very different recollection is that the job had fallen to Camp only because she had not been able to get to the studio on the day the vocal was to be recorded. In any case, knowing that Dunford often composed specifically for Haslam's voice, one can only wonder what the piece might have sounded like had she sung it.

'Northern Lights' 4:07 (Dunford/Thatcher)

The band's sole monster hit single (top-ten in the UK), this irresistibly melodic pop song is not, contrary to popular belief, about the Aurora Borealis. Rather, the 'northern lights' of the song's title are the northern lights of England. The origins of the song lay in Haslam's confession to her friend, lyricist Thatcher, that she would often become homesick during the band's many concert tours of the US, especially missing her fiancé, musician Roy Wood, who was back home in England. Thatcher converted this information into lyrics like these:

> You know it's hard away from you
> Travelling roads and passing through
> It's not for money and it's not for fame
> I just can't explain
> Sometimes it's lonely

Despite the tone of those lines, 'Northern Lights' is an unmistakably happy song. The tune is bouncy and cheerful, and Haslam's vocal sounds buoyant, perhaps because the song is not just about leaving and being homesick, but also about the joy of returning home. This is brought out clearly in the infectious chorus: 'The northern lights are in my mind/ They guide me back to you/ The northern nights are in my eyes/ They guide me back to you'. And the dubious claim that Haslam' just can't explain' why she goes away, since 'It's not for money and it's not for fame', is contradicted twice in the song by her declaration, sung with joyful exuberance, that 'now I live to sing'.

The arrangement is simple but effective and appealing. Dunford's strummed twelve-string acoustic guitar, possibly multi-tracked, as it sounds massive, establishes the rhythm, at first assisted only by Camp's high-in-the-mix bubbling bass lines, Tout's occasional synthesizer flourishes, and Sullivan's even more infrequent roto-tom drum and tambourine strikes. At two points Dunford takes a break from his rhythmic strumming, as Tout and Camp replace it with a delightful baroque-style duet in counterpoint to Haslam's vocal. At the conclusion of the first of these two passages, Sullivan re-enters with a more committed drum statement, and this time stays in to assist rhythmically as Dunford resumes his strumming duties.

The vocal arrangement becomes progressively more involved as the track unfolds, as Haslam first sings alone, than doubles (or triples) herself through multi-tracking, then harmonises with herself through overdubbing, then does so with her voices staggered, so as to create counterpoint, and then finally is joined by Camp's voice, also staggered.

At the conclusion of a glorious rendition of the chorus, the song threatens to come to an end. But Sullivan's brief drum fill, quickly followed by a Camp bass lick, starts it up again, leading to a most welcome return of the chorus, which is then repeated two or three times as the track fades out.

The band had wanted a hit single, and with 'Northern Lights' they got it, in a triumph that was richly deserved. But sometimes success of that sort can be a curse, as it can tempt a band into trying in vain to repeat it, often at the cost of losing focus on their artistic vision, and forgetting what it is that they do best.

'A Song For All Seasons' 10:55 (Camp/Dunford/Thatcher/Tout/Sullivan)

And speaking of what the band does best, this brings us to the album closer, the title track, perhaps the heaviest, moodiest, and most dramatic piece in the Renaissance catalogue.

Its subject matter is elemental, like a secular version of the book of Genesis in the Bible, as it refers to the four seasons in the context of discussing the beginning of time and the most basic aspects of human existence. Thus, the first verse, addressing spring and summer, includes all of the following words: 'time', 'wind', 'earth', 'fire', 'air', 'water', 'sea', 'landscape', 'purpose', 'meaning', 'changing', and 'roots'.

The second verse, on autumn, winter, and then (once again) spring, speaks of 'the past and the future, holding together', of 'changes', and of the need for 'learning' and 'planning'. Both verses end with these words: 'These are our roots, and it's our way/ We grow, we reap, and sow/ We reap and sow the seasons of our day'.

The last vocal section, sung to a different melody than that of the verses, mentions the four directions, 'North', 'South', 'East', and 'West', speaks of humans' crawling', and then 'flying', and then concludes by boldly (and correctly, in my opinion) placing music at this same elemental level, proudly asserting the fundamental and essential importance to human existence of what they, as musicians, do.

The piece ends with these words:

Man has music
Man has North, South, East and West
Man makes music
A song for all seasons through

Song for all seasons
A song for all our time
We'll have a song for all the seasons through

Statements as grand as these call for equally audacious music and that is supplied here, in abundance, as the band and orchestra cast off all restraints – a surprise, given the band's general tendency, especially in the hands of Tout, Dunford, and Sullivan, for moderation, subtlety, and understatement. The arrangement is unusually rich and dynamic, as the track undergoes many changes of key, tempo, volume, and instrumentation, with seemingly every instrument in the band and orchestra being at some point spotlighted, however briefly.

The instrumental introduction, containing many of the shifts just mentioned, is substantial, as electronic keyboards, bass, drums, xylophone, strings, horns, piano, and acoustic guitar all vie for attention for nearly four minutes, playing moody music, mostly on the stormy, aggressive, percussive side, prior to the entrance of Haslam's lead vocal. Notice, for example, the episode beginning three minutes in, in which Tout's quiet piano is angrily interrupted by loud string and horn statements, which are in turn punctuated by declamatory drum and cymbal strikes, all at maximum volume, communicating a message of maximum urgency, which is further underscored by the dramatic gong strike that effectively ends the episode.

A quiet pattern, which will serve as the initial background for Haslam's vocal, emerges from the decay of the gong strike, featuring acoustic guitar, bass, celeste, and electronic keyboard strings. She sings softly over it at first. But then a brief instrumental crescendo leads to a new, rocking, background. With the orchestra and band now fully engaged, Haslam's vocal also takes on a new power and enthusiasm. Entirely consistent with the shifting dynamics of the entire track, this exciting episode lasts only eighteen seconds, as the intensity ratchets down, only to creep back up again toward the end of the verse, reaching a climax as Haslam, who harmonises with herself for the first time on the last line of the verse ('We reap and sow the seasons of our day'), leaps up to a high E note on 'day', leading to a thunderous response by the band and orchestra, in a recapitulation of the passage first heard two minutes earlier.

The inconsistencies of dynamics in this first verse are matched by equally striking harmonic instabilities, as the band finds a way to use chords that are beautiful, interesting, and affecting, even though they are, strictly speaking, off-key.

The instrumentation changes a bit for the second verse, as this time we hear, during its initial, quieter, part, strings, an English horn, and (immediately following that) a beautiful, soaring flute line. Still, the dynamic and harmonic patterns remain the same here as they were in the first verse.

The second verse then gives way to a new instrumental section. It begins with a quiet acoustic guitar, piano, and strings episode. As other instruments, including gorgeous horns, then a warm English horn/bassoon duet, join in this peaceful passage, the volume gradually increases, before taking a big jump in loudness, setting the stage for the final vocal section. Here Haslam sings of crawling, flying, the four directions, and 'a song for all seasons', to a melody clearly derived from the thunderous instrumental passage, first heard three minutes in and subsequently repeated at the end of each of the first two verses. While this passage had sounded angry and ominous then, here it sounds intense, earnest, and purposeful, but more proud and defiant than angry.

The conclusion of this vocal stanza leads to a lengthy, highly melodic, instrumental passage, in which the tune is carried primarily, at first, by the surprising combination of bass and celeste, and subsequently by strings. This passage, fairly hot and involved at the outset, eventually adds horns to the mix and continually gains in power and volume as it proceeds.

At the conclusion of this episode, Haslam returns to sing the song's final lines, quoted above, about music. The intensity ratchets up as Haslam, on the final word of the song's penultimate line, 'A song for all our time', leaps up to hit an astonishing G5 note, only to top it, at the end of the final line, 'We'll have a song for all the seasons through', with a mind-blowing B5.

At the conclusion of this breath-taking climax, the orchestra decelerates for a few seconds before loudly striking the E minor chord that brings the track, and the album, to a triumphant close.

A Song for All Seasons, Renaissance's best-selling album to date, was to be the band's last album of the twentieth-century to include long, multi-section, classically-inspired pieces, such as this album's title track and 'Day of the Dreamer'.

Azure D'Or (1979)

Personnel:
Jon Camp: bass, vocals, bass pedals, electric and twelve-string acoustic guitars, cello
Michael Dunford: electric, classical, and twelve-string acoustic guitars, autoharp, mandolin
Annie Haslam: vocals
Terry Sullivan: drums, small percussion, vocals, timpani, chimes, glockenspiel, gong, kalimba, xylophone
John Tout: piano, synths, Mellotron, electric piano, organ, clavinet
Producer: David Hentschel
Release date: June 1979
Highest chart position: 73 (UK), 125 (US)
Running time of original LP: 42:57

When Renaissance returned to the recording studio to make a follow-up to *A Song for All Seasons*, they might have attempted to replicate the formula that had proved so successful for that album. After all, it had been the band's best selling album to date and had also yielded their first hit single. But instead of going for the balance between old and new that they had achieved there, with a couple of proggy epics to balance the new, shorter songs, and the presence of an orchestra to balance the new emphasis on electric guitars and synthesizers, the band opted to go further in the direction of these new elements, and to leave the past behind. Thus, in *Azure d'Or* we have an accelerated reliance on synthesizers, and no orchestra at all, coupled with a complete abandoning of the band's trademark extended, multi-section pieces, replaced by a total commitment to short, poppy tracks with simple, unchallenging song structures, and, in many cases, dance rhythms. *Azure d'Or* would feature just one track exceeding five minutes in length, and even that one would not clear the barrier by much, clocking in at just 5:13.

Had the melodies of these new, shorter, songs matched the standard set by the band's output of the 1972-1977 period, this change of direction might have worked out, as Renaissance had already proven, with 'Carpet of the Sun', 'The Vultures Fly High', and the recent 'Northern Lights', to be capable of producing short-form works of excellent quality. But instead, the decline in ambition was matched by a decline in execution, as the merely OK-to-fairly-good quality of the melodies led to a disappointing album – still decent, still containing many enjoyable moments, definitely not a disaster, but nonetheless quite a comedown from the heights of the *Prologue* to *Novella* sequence. As Dunford would later, quite bluntly, put it, 'The songs weren't as good'.

'Jekyll And Hyde' 4:38 (Dunford/Thatcher)
The album does get off to a flying start, however, with this extremely catchy rocker, the bouncy melodies of which stand in contrast to the darkness of its lyrical subject matter. It concerns a man with a dual personality, one of which

is very good, the other horribly bad. Such a man is described most famously in Robert Louis Stevenson's 1866 novella, *Strange Case of Dr Jekyll and Mr Hyde*, leading to the phrase 'Jekyll and Hyde' entering the vernacular to refer to people of this sort.

Though the arrangement lacks the tempo and dynamics changes that the band has used effectively in the past, it is otherwise very good. The instrumental backing track sizzles from start to finish; Haslam sings beautifully, sometimes accompanied by Camp, and at other times harmonising with herself; and Tout provides an outstanding solo in the middle, the first part bold and powerful, the latter part more tuneful, and with a dreamy quality.

But what really makes the song is the quality of the vocal melodies. There are three of them here: the 'Duplicated man' verse, heard twice; the three iterations, each with different lyrics, of stanzas beginning with 'This man'; and the 'Deep down inside' chorus – and all three are excellent. Though each one is repeated, and in the case of the latter two, repeated more than once, one is glad to hear each melody again, every time it comes around.

If every song on the album had been as strong as this one, the band's change in direction might have been judged a success.

'The Winter Tree' 3:02 (Dunford/Thatcher)

Haslam reports that in preparing this album the band had been asked to write something commercial, 'so we came up with 'The Winter Tree'.' In Haslam's view that was a 'great commercial-sounding song', but 'it was left too long before it came out', with the result that the single was not a commercial success. 'Then we started to lose our way after that musically and it just fell apart, really'.

It's a pleasant track, elevated by the quality of Haslam's vocal, but also rather bland and inconsequential. The lyrics take up one of Thatcher's favourite themes, the joys of nature, in this case, those of the warm sunshine in spring and summer. She seems to be exhorting us to cheer up if we find winter depressing, in such lines as 'Though your mind may hold the wintertime/ Spring is never very far behind', or the refrain, 'Take it easy live today, today/ We'll see the sunshine, shine on'. The music, though certainly unobjectionable, is similarly lightweight. The absence of exciting musical twists and turns is keenly felt.

'Only Angels Have Wings' 3:43 (Camp)

A Camp composition, on which he takes the lead vocal, this one suffers from the minimal and monotonous nature of the instrumental backing track. The band essentially does not play. Neither drums, bass, nor guitar are heard (Sullivan and Dunford make no appearance.) There is no orchestra. Tout does not play piano, by far his best instrument. And Haslam is only faintly heard, occasionally supplying background harmony.

So the accompaniment to Camp's vocal boils down to Tout, on electronic keyboards, trying in vain to simulate a small orchestra. While he is undoubtedly an outstanding musician and makes a valiant effort here, he seems not to be quite up to this particular task. The part he plays is too simple and too repetitious to be interesting or appealing, and (though this is not his fault) it is placed too high in the mix. Moreover, the spare nature of the instrumental accompaniment causes more of a spotlight to be shown on Camp's music, lyrics, and singing. While his singing can bear that scrutiny, the tune and the words stand in need of some help if they are to catch fire – help which, unfortunately, they do not receive.

'Golden Key' 5:13 (Dunford/Thatcher)

Ironically, rock albums of the 1980s tend to sound much more dated today than do albums of the early- or mid-1970s. The reason is that in the 1980s musicians and producers became so fascinated by the new sound production techniques that were made possible by the technology that was emerging at that time – synthesizers, drum machines, sequencers, and the like – that they lost sight of the human element, and created recordings that sounded heavily processed, cold, mechanical, and robotic. Though *Azure d'Or* was released in 1979, its production moves in this direction – an unfortunate change for Renaissance, a band that had been celebrated for its clear, uncluttered, open, inviting, unprocessed, very human, sound, which it achieved in part by tending to use low-tech, primarily acoustic, untreated instruments (acoustic guitar over electric guitar; piano over electronic keyboards; and strings, woodwinds, and brass played by human beings in an orchestra, rather than simulated by means of a synthesizer).

This track, by means of the contrast between its cold, precise, heavily processed-sounding introduction, on the one hand, and the warm, human quality that emerges when Haslam enters to sing the first verse, accompanied solely by Tout's piano, on the other, throws this production-driven change in the band's sound into sharp relief.

The melody that she sings, while not one of Dunford's best (a very high standard), is good, and one is happy to hear it repeated when Haslam immediately moves on to the second verse.

Here the band adopts its standard arranging technique of increasing the instrumental backing by having the individual players join in, one or two at a time, thus highlighting the complexity of the layering of the different parts. This approach works well here and makes for an appealing contrast to the simpler, piano-only, accompaniment of the first verse, which is also effective and enjoyable.

But the volume then increases as Haslam segues to the chorus, and this, coupled with the now much more prominent faux-orchestral synthesizer line in the background, gives this part an unpleasantly blaring quality. This is exacerbated by the awkwardness of the chorus's vocal melody, which compares unfavourably to that of the verses.

The chorus gives way to a fairly substantial instrumental section – a real rarity on this album, but a most welcome one. It begins quietly, as Tout plays a simple, but catchy, synthesizer melody, accompanying himself on another keyboard, before being joined by Dunford on his acoustic twelve-string guitar. Sullivan's drums and Camp's bass then kick in, as the track increasingly takes on a rock band feel. Sullivan and Camp establish an urgent-sounding accent pattern, in which they emphasize the first two half-beats of each 4/4 measure while deemphasising the remaining three beats. As the track progressively gains volume and intensity, one also begins to hear background singing, in 'ah' vocalise. While this sounds good, and so, on balance, counts as a positive, it is disappointing that the voices sound either completely artificial, the result of a keyboard patch, or, at the very least, heavily processed.

The completion of this instrumental section leads immediately to Haslam's rendition of the third verse, followed by a reiteration of the chorus. The song ends on a brief, but lovely, outro – Tout softly reprising the first part of the verse melody on piano, joined, at the very end, by a few well-chosen notes from Camp's bass.

Forever Changing 4:48 (Sullivan/Thatcher)

This is the only song in the Renaissance catalogue for which Sullivan is credited as the sole composer. (He had received just one other co-writing credit, being listed as one of the four composers of 'A Song for All Seasons'. Thatcher's credit, on both songs, is for lyrics.)

Haslam takes the lead vocal, and sounds great, as usual. But the melody falls far short of the Dunford standard, and Thatcher has written better lyrics in other songs about this song's subject matter – being outdoors in the 'forever changing' seasons.

The arrangement is somewhat interesting. The instrumental accompaniment to Haslam's singing is dominated by an unusually thickly-textured acoustic guitar sound, featuring both Camp and Dunford on twelve-strings, with Dunford also contributing classical guitar and autoharp parts. Sullivan also makes use of an unusually varied set of percussion instruments, including timpani, glockenspiel, and kalimba.

'Secret Mission' 5:00 (Camp)

Both starting off and ending with rapid-fire solo drumming from Sullivan, and featuring Camp's upfront lead-guitar style bass riffs, this rocking Camp composition seems designed to show off the band's rhythm section.

Camp wisely hands off the lead vocal duties to Haslam, who makes the most of his fairly good verse melody and unremarkable chorus.

Tout's synthesizer sound is a bit cheesy for much of the tune, but improves in the impressive coda, in which the band turns in a very creditable Emerson, Lake & Palmer impression.

'Kalynda (A Magical Isle)' 3:43 (Camp)

Though it never truly catches fire, this is a pleasant mid-tempo tune. Its structure could not be more straightforward: two verses, chorus, third verse, final chorus, framed by an extremely minimal intro and outro, and with no substantial instrumental sections interrupting the transitions among verses and choruses.

Like 'Forever Changing', the instrumental backing leans heavily on acoustic guitar, with Camp adding some nice, relaxed-sounding electric guitar lead lines here and there.

Haslam takes the lead vocal and performs up to her usual high standard.

The rather bland lyrics appear to be about wanting to be on a special Island – much like the song 'Island', from the very first Renaissance album.

'The Discovery' 4:23 (Camp)

This instrumental (there is no singing at all, not even wordless vocalise) comes closer to a progressive rock style than any other track on the album.

It begins with the sound of ocean waves (which probably explains its placement right after 'Kalynda', as that song had ended with such sounds, appropriate to its island theme). The ocean sounds continue for about 50 seconds, over which we hear the occasional striking of chords on some kind of electronic keyboard, accompanied by what appear to be wind chimes.

The band then comes in, with Tout playing a tuneful electronic keyboard lick over an up-tempo rock backing. In spite of the lack of singing, the piece is structured very much like a song, with distinct, alternating melodic parts, much in the same manner as a verses/chorus distinction. The band transitions from verse to chorus, back to verse, and then to chorus again.

The basis for the progressive rock designation emerges more clearly over the track's final two minutes, as it packs three new instrumental sections into that time period, each at a different tempo, in a different style, and with a different feel.

First, the tempo slows down, as either Camp or Dunford takes the lead on electric guitar, soloing over Sullivan's aggressive drumming (he bashes a cymbal on every downbeat). This transitions to a much faster section, in which one of the guitarists, employing a tone much different from that of the previous section, plays a delightful Spanish-flavoured, classical-sounding, solo, against a background in which, once again, Sullivan's frenetic drumming is the standout element.

This leads to the final section – a menacing passage that borders on a heavy metal style.

Though one misses Haslam's voice, this Camp composition skilfully integrates its several distinct, contrasting sections, into a consistently interesting and enjoyable whole, making it one of the album's more successful tracks.

'Friends' 3:30 (Dunford/Thatcher)

Songs don't get much simpler, or more repetitive, than this. Thatcher's lyrics essentially boil down to the idea that friendship is a very good thing –

not exactly a bold or challenging thesis. And the song's structure is equally straightforward: verse, chorus, verse, chorus, repeat chorus, then twice repeat the latter half of the chorus as the tune fades out. In the absence of any significant instrumental sections, the instrumentation just serves the function of accompanying the vocals.

The vocal melodies are serviceable, pleasant enough as they're sliding by, but not at all striking or memorable. The song's assets include some nice acoustic twelve-string strumming from Dunford, Camp's funky, trebly bass line, Haslam's lead vocal, and the choral effect (Haslam multi-tracked, plus Camp) on the chorus – but even these are somewhat diminished by the way in which their sound is altered by the antiseptic, overly processed 1980s-style production.

This is a harmless, inconsequential, little tune, not likely to give offence – unless one recalls, while listening to it, that it was made by the same people who once brought you 'Ashes Are Burning', 'Mother Russia', 'Can You Hear Me?', and 'A Song for All Seasons'.

'The Flood At Lyons' 4:57 (Camp/Dunford)

All six of the previous Haslam-era albums had ended with a serious, weighty, epic. Here the band seems to be trying for a similar effect in the compass of a shorter song.

The subject matter for this album closer is certainly serious – a flood, here used poetically to represent loss, a larger, more general and abstract, theme. And the dazzling stop-and-start xylophone episode in the song's introductory section suggests that we are about to hear something fresh and creative, rather than another song with a safe, conventional, by-the-numbers structure and arrangement.

But as the track unfolds, it becomes clear that the device chosen for conveying the weight of its subject matter is to embed the song's melody (one of merely adequate tunefulness) within a thick, orchestra-plus-choir style arrangement. While this might well have worked with a real orchestra, and with either a real choir or the multi-tracked voices of Haslam and Camp, it falls completely flat with the cheesy, electronically simulated orchestra and choir that was in fact used.

Haslam's vocal performance is excellent, and Sullivan's injection of chimes into the mix of the faux orchestral outro is a very nice touch.

Thus ends the disappointing *Azure d'Or* – not a terrible album, to be sure, but in every sense the least successful one of the Haslam era to this point. (It charted higher upon release than some of the earlier albums had done, but all of them have since surpassed it in sales as a result of re-releases and back catalogue purchases.) It would turn out to be the last album made by the 'classic' Renaissance line-up of Camp, Dunford, Haslam, Sullivan, and Tout. In spite of going out on a sour note, these players have a right to be proud of the (almost) uniformly high quality of their very substantial (seven studio albums, several live albums, and hundreds of concert appearances) contribution to the world of music. There is evidence that this contribution will be a lasting one, as the classic albums continue to be re-released in new, expanded editions, nearly fifty years after they were made.

Related Track
'Island Of Avalon' 2:46 (Dunford/Thatcher)

A non-album B-side, this was paired with 'The Winter Tree' as the first single off *Azure d'Or*. It has subsequently been released on the 1997 compilation CD, *Songs from Renaissance Days*, a collection of B-sides, demos, and other unreleased recordings made between 1979 and the mid-1980s.

Although the vocal melody is not particularly compelling, otherwise this is an enjoyable track – more so than many others that made it onto the album. Unlike much of the *Azure d'Or* album, it does not suffer from 1980s-style production techniques, and the arrangement, dominated by rapid acoustic guitar strumming, is simple and uncluttered, thus letting Haslam's voice shine through as the dominant element in the soundscape. The lyrics are about the legendary island of Arthurian legend.

Camera Camera (1981)

Personnel:
Jon Camp: bass, backing vocals, electric guitar
Michael Dunford: acoustic and electric guitars, backing vocals
Annie Haslam: vocals
Peter Barron: drums, percussion, backing vocals
Peter Gosling: keyboards, backing vocals
Producer: Renaissance
Release date: 1981
Highest chart position: 196 (US)
Running time of original LP: 45:01 (The CD version is slightly longer, as the fade out ending is extended a bit on several tracks.)
Note: The song 'Bonjour Swansong' was left off the original 1981 release, but has been included on every one of the album's several subsequent releases, beginning in 1982. The running time given above is for the releases that include 'Bonjour Swansong'.

In 1980, following the release of the disappointing *Azure D'Or*, it was clear that Renaissance was a band in decline, both commercially and artistically. Why did this happen? How could a group that had established such a consistent record of excellence from 1972-1977 fall as far from that standard by 1979 as it did?

In order to answer that question, it is helpful to begin by recognising how difficult it is for any group of musicians to work together cooperatively, making personal sacrifices for the good of the group, over an extended period of time. So many things can go wrong: members can die, or quit, or become quarrelsome and uncooperative; disagreements about artistic direction can become insurmountable; jealousy and resentment can develop as some members receive more recognition than others; there can be disputes over money; and so on.

Moreover, even if a band successfully avoids pitfalls of this sort, there are built-in obstacles to the achievement of commercial viability over time. For one thing, in order to sustain commercial success, it is imperative to attract new audiences, since a band is always in the process of losing audience members who either die or, through changes in their life circumstances, no longer have the money and/or time necessary for buying albums and concert tickets. But in trying to attract new audiences, it is also important to hang on to as much of the old audience as possible. Thus arises the problem of striking the right balance between continuity and change. To reach new audiences, it might be necessary for a band to make changes, so as to keep up with contemporary tastes, and to attract listeners who had not warmed to the band's earlier offerings. But therein lies the dilemma: change too much, and you run the risk of alienating the audience that likes the sound and style you've already established; but change too little, and you risk having that audience reject your new output, based on their conclusion that it offers nothing that is not already available in the older works.

With this in mind, I suggest that five factors led to the late 1970s decline of Renaissance.

First of all, the general pressure to stay current was exacerbated at this time by rapid changes in popular music tastes. Progressive rock was going out of style, yielding to new wave, punk, disco, and synth-pop, among other newer genres. But Renaissance was very good at making classically-influenced, multi-section epics, and not nearly as good at working in any of these newer styles. It is noteworthy, in this connection, that other progressive rock bands, including Genesis, Yes, and Emerson, Lake & Palmer, also compromised their classic styles at this time, moving more in the direction of newer trends. In doing so, they, like Renaissance, created some of their weakest albums.

Secondly, prior to 1978, Renaissance had very much been an album-oriented band. But they scored a top-ten single that year with 'Northern Lights', which was a short pop song, rather than a specimen of progressive rock. Further, the single presumably helped with album sales, as the album on which 'Northern Lights' appeared, *A Song for All Seasons*, outsold each of the band's many previous efforts. This, even apart from any consideration of market changes, may have persuaded some of the band members that the path of shorter, simpler songs was the better one going forward. Perhaps more importantly, their record company took this position. As Haslam explains it, 'We had a hit with 'Northern Lights', and that's when we were encouraged to write more commercial music. We did a turnaround musically instead of trying to take our music into the 1980s'. Camp concurs: 'We were under a lot of pressure from Warner Brothers in England to emulate the success of 'Northern Lights' as a single. They thought we had more life in us over here with regard to getting hit singles to chart in the United Kingdom'.

Thirdly, largely because of their use of orchestras, Renaissance's 1973-1978 albums were expensive to make. Record companies were constantly on the lookout for ways to save on expenses. The huge success of 'Northern Lights', coupled with the recent arrival of cheaper orchestra-simulating keyboards, may have persuaded Renaissance's record company that the band could make hits without the cost of hiring an orchestra and an orchestral arranger. This may explain the absence of an orchestra on *Azure d'Or*. And that absence, in turn, undoubtedly contributed to some of the problems with that album. For one thing, even in the best of circumstances, a synthesizer-simulated orchestra does not sound as good as an orchestra. For another, the task of artificially manufacturing orchestra sounds could not help but take Tout away from his major strength (and a major part of the band's classic sound), the piano. Finally, though this is speculative, the unavailability of an orchestra may have negatively influenced the compositions for the album. With no orchestra, there would be less point in preparing material that would be best played by one. Thus, there would be an impetus to write simpler, poppier, less demanding pieces.

Fourthly, though the members of the classic 1972-1979 incarnation of Renaissance have avoided criticising each other, or airing internal grievances, publicly, one can detect in some of their comments that the question of musical direction caused divisions within the band in the late 1970s, as some favoured moving in the direction of newer musical trends, while others wanted to stay the course. It seems likely that this disunity would have exerted a negative effect on the band's musical output, in part because it likely resulted in some of the members having to make a contribution to music for which they had little enthusiasm.

Finally, it often isn't recognised how rigorous the life of a touring and recording rock band was in the 1970s. Renaissance put out seven studio albums in the 1972-1979 period, averaging one per year. That meant a constant grind of making an album in the studio (a lengthy and laborious process), and then going out on concert tours to promote it (thus enduring the fatiguing and mind-numbing ordeal of constant travel, coupled with the great hardship of being away from home, separated from loved ones), and then going back into the studio again, as the process continued endlessly. It is almost impossible not to be worn down by such a life – to become tired, to lose enthusiasm, to be ready for a change. This could be expected to affect the music directly, as it is easier, especially for musicians suffering from an energy and/or enthusiasm deficit, to write, arrange, and perform, short, simple songs, of average quality, than it is to struggle and strain in an effort to write excellent musical sections, and then to put in the work of compiling them into complicated, well-coordinated pieces of considerable length.

As if this were not bad enough, two negative events, of such significance as to threaten the continued existence of the band, occurred in 1980. The first was the departure of two of the band's five members, John Tout and Terry Sullivan. Tout, in a state of emotional distress due to the death of his sister, had made a major mistake during a concert performance and then had compounded his error by walking offstage in response, thus abandoning his bandmates for the remainder of the concert. As a result, he either was fired or else decided it was best that he resign (accounts differ). When Sullivan, whose deep friendship with Tout predated their joining forces in Renaissance, found out about this, he decided to quit as well. As he explains it in a recent interview, this was partly due to his regarding Tout as 'the very heart of the Renaissance sound', but also was motivated by 'the fact that I was spending all my time travelling, supporting albums from which I made very little'. (He quickly adds that he has no hard feelings now, 'as time heals'.)

The second major negative event was the decision of the band's label, Warner Brothers/Sire, to drop the group in response to the poor sales performance of *Azure d'Or*.

In the wake of these disasters, it was at first unclear whether Renaissance, which had undergone personnel changes in the past, would do so again and continue as a working band. The prospects for this initially appeared unpromising, as Dunford and Haslam promptly formed a new, three-piece, group, called 'Nevada', with keyboardist Peter Gosling. They released a couple of singles under that name and recorded several demos.

However, when given the opportunity to sign on, as Renaissance, to IRS Records, the label that their former manager, Miles Copeland, had recently founded, Dunford and Haslam reunited with Camp in order to do so, thus reconstituting Renaissance as a three-piece band.

To help them on their first IRS album, Dunford and Haslam brought in their Nevada band mate Gosling, on keyboards, with the drummer position going to Peter Barron. But Gosling and Barron were to be credited only as guest musicians, as it is noteworthy that the only persons pictured on the *Camera Camera* cover were the trio, Haslam, Dunford, and Camp.

From *Prologue* through *Novella*, and for a good portion of *A Song for All Seasons*, Renaissance's sound had been unique, utterly unlike that of any other band. The key ingredients had been: Haslam's voice, Dunford's beautiful, classically-inspired melodies, the band's skill at arranging, and navigating lengthy, multi-section song structures, and the group's distinctive instrumentation – acoustic guitar, acoustic piano, and orchestration. Starting with a few songs on *A Song for All Seasons*, and increasingly on *Azure d'Or*, all these elements except Haslam's voice began to decline, so that by the time of *Camera Camera* they were almost entirely absent. The quality of Dunford's melodies declined; the band opted for shorter, more conventionally structured songs; and they relied more on electric guitar and electronic keyboards, and ditched the orchestra. As Dunford would later put it, 'it was the wrong direction for us'.

'Camera Camera' 6:02 (Camp/Dunford)

The album opener is the title track, the story of a model, a role that Haslam impersonates by singing about her in the first person.

The track begins with a sound effect, the sound of camera shutters rapidly opening and closing. The band then jumps in, starting with Camp's bass and Gosling's electronic keyboard, shortly followed by Barron's drums and Dunford's insistent, trebly electric guitar riff. The band sounds tight, as they establish an up-tempo groove – though they don't sound anything like Renaissance. If anything, they sound a good deal like the Police, their new label mates, managed by their former manager and current label boss, Miles Copeland, brother of the Police's drummer, Stewart Copeland. For example, the brief passage which sets up the entrance of Haslam's lead vocal is strongly reminiscent of the Police's 1979 hit, 'Message in a Bottle'.

Haslam's singing is unusual here, in that she sings in character, as a model who is 'lovely to look at and lovely to hold', but with a 'spirit that's broken and a heart that's ice-cold', and accordingly adopts an uncharacteristically arrogant and chilly tone. Moreover, at the beginning of the second and fourth line of both verses, she leaps up from a B4 note to a G5, hitting it with a high, chirping quaver, unlike anything ever heard on any previous Renaissance recording.

More vocal gymnastics are to be found at the end of each chorus, where

Haslam holds its final note, on the word 'cold', for a total of thirteen seconds on its first iteration, and eighteen seconds on its second.

An oddity in the song is that Haslam inexplicably switches from the first-person perspective that has been in play from the beginning of the song, with consistent usage of 'I' and 'me' when referring to the model, to a third-person perspective in the song's final line: 'You know she nearly made it, but she had a child instead'.

The track closes out on a moderately lengthy instrumental section, dominated by Dunford's electric guitar and Gosling's synths.

'Faeries (Living At The Bottom Of The Garden)' 4:00 (Dunford/ Gosling)

The sole song on the album for which Gosling received a writing credit, this track began life as part of the Nevada project, as it is a new version of a song that had been recorded as a demo by that short-lived band.

The song is presumably about a real historical event, as the phrase 'faeries at the bottom of the garden' generally refers to a well-publicised event from 1917, in which two cousins, Elsie Wright and Frances Griffiths, aged sixteen and nine, took a series of photographs purportedly showing themselves cavorting with faeries at the bottom of a garden near the village of Cottingley in the UK. Though the photos were fakes, and rather obvious ones at that (the faeries were cardboard cut-outs), they fooled the famous writer, Arthur Conan Doyle, a man whose mental acuity utterly failed to rival that of his famous creation, Sherlock Holmes. Doyle publicised and defended the photos, setting off a public debate over their authenticity.

The most interesting thing about Renaissance's song about this incident is that it features a lead vocal in which Haslam, just as she had done in the album opener, changes her singing style so as to sing in character, in the first person. Here she takes on the persona of one of the young girls, and thus sings in a childish voice.

A bland, nondescript tune, performed competently, in a new wave-ish, synth-pop style, it benefits from Camp's chunky bass line but suffers from far too many repetitions of its only moderately catchy chorus.

'Remember' 4:28 (Dunford/Thatcher)

A song about the importance of keeping letters and photographs, so as to remember loved ones who have died (in this case, in war), this one is marred by music that drains Thatcher's lyrics of the poignancy they have when simply read on the page.

It starts promisingly, as the band opts for its tried-and-true, layer-in-the-instruments-one-at-a-time, approach. Barron's short drum solo starts it off, soon to be joined by Gosling's keyboards, Dunford's electric guitar, and Camp's bass, in that order. But the cheerful, carefree backing groove that they create, which is decent enough if taken on its own terms, clashes with the much more serious emotive content of Thatcher's lyrics – a complaint that also applies to Dunford's rather weightless melody.

The song's structure is simple and straightforward: brief intro, two verses, chorus, third verse, final chorus, then a lengthy (about 90 seconds), pointless, repetitive outro, featuring a series of obnoxious synthesizer noises.

'Bonjour Swansong' 3:37 (Dunford/Thatcher)

Long-time Renaissance lyricist Betty Thatcher wrote lyrics to just four songs on *Camera Camera*, and then took a long break from writing lyrics for Renaissance, because, as she explains, 'I'd become disenchanted with the outlook of the group when I wrote this ('Bonjour Swansong'). They were looking for a follow up single and said things like, 'We should be more like Genesis'. I thought the whole motivation of classical rock had been abandoned. I wrote 'Bonjour Swansong' as my private goodbye to the group'.

It is an affectionate farewell, as Thatcher does not point fingers or lay blame on anyone, but rather simply expresses regret that the affair, of sorts, was over ('I could have loved you longer/ Over all too soon'), and gratitude for the sweet memories it had given her ('And I thought we'd touch eternity/ But all we have are memories/ I thank you for the sweetness/ That you gave to me').

The problem, as with the previous track, is that the music is blandly cheerful, and fails to convey the bittersweet emotion of Thatcher's lyrics.

For some reason, 'Bonjour Swansong' was left off the original 1981 LP release of *Camera Camera* in the UK. But it has been restored on all subsequent releases, starting the next year.

'Tyrant-Tula' 5:58 (Camp/Dunford)

This is a song about political oppression. It speaks of people who suffer at the hands of the 'tyrant' of the song's title. But the lyrics are vague, leaving it unclear what the particular issues are in this case, and whether the tyrant's victims are refugees leaving his domain, or revolutionaries, working to overthrow him.

In any case, the main problem here is the same as the one mentioned with regard to the two immediately preceding tracks – the lyrics are about something serious, and have emotive content, but are not matched with music that conveys that sense of seriousness or communicates that emotive content.

The music here, considered apart from the lyrics, is not without interest. The track begins with a catchy electric guitar riff that is reprised repeatedly throughout the piece, and at one point taken up effectively by Camp on bass. And unlike most songs on this album, this one has a couple of entertaining instrumental sections. One, beginning at just before three minutes, works in a lot of variety, as it transitions from a bass riff to a brief dance rhythms bit, to some spacey synthesizer sounds, and then to some nice piano runs, before returning us to the last part of Haslam's fine lead vocal. And the fairly extensive outro features some intriguing drumming and sound effects.

But, in common with most of the songs on the album, the vocal melodies are merely serviceable – far from the Dunford standard of 1972-1977.

'Okichi-San' 5:58 (Dunford/Thatcher)

The story of a geisha, this leisurely-paced, acoustic guitar-based, atmospheric track tries to sound Japanese. It benefits from a Haslam high-pitched vocalise sequence (near the beginning of the song) and from an effectively moody outro. Despite another just fair vocal melody, this is enough to make it, on balance, one of the most engaging tracks on the album.

'Jigsaw' 5:05 (Dunford/Thatcher)

A fairly convincing rocker, this one features Thatcher's take on the band's confusion about how to move forward in the aftermath of the failure of *Azure D'or*. Haslam, singing in her lower register (going all the way down to an F3), sums it up convincingly at the song's end:

> Here in the centre of an endless hazy maze
> I know I lost the way and I don't know nights from days
> And now there's no solution
> I know that I can't use all the confusion, all the
>
> Jigsaws, all that I ever see
> Unsure where I want to be
> See-saw, you standing next to me
> The edges of my days are all astray

On the last syllable of 'astray' (which occurs at the end of the thrice-sung chorus), Haslam slides into a kind of scream, landing on an A5 note – a startling effect, given that she is operating more than two octaves lower than that in the verses.

The instrumental passages work well here. A substantial piano-led introduction starts it off, with Dunford's guitar, playing chunky chords, followed by Camp's loud, trebly, lead-guitar style bass, setting the stage for the beginning of Haslam's lead vocal.

Also noteworthy is Camp's bass solo in the middle of the song and Gosling's electronic keyboard solo, which follows it. Camp's thunderous bass riff, then returns the track to the vocal sections.

While the vocal melodies still fall far short of Dunford's 1972-1977 standard, they are among the best on this album. Moreover, the band manages to rock out without sounding cheesy or robotic. And, most importantly, here the music stands as an aid, rather than an obstacle, to the communication of the emotion inherent in Thatcher's lyrics.

'Running Away From You' 3:51 (Camp)

It is difficult to find the right words to describe this repetitive synth-pop track, which, as one reviewer commented, 'has an almost appalling one-two dance beat, fingernails-on-chalkboard synths, and insipid lyrics that are far beneath the dignity of someone of Haslam's musical stature'.

'Ukraine Ways' 6:26 (Camp/Dunford)

A Russian-sounding piece, somewhat in the tradition of 'Kiev' and 'Mother Russia', this Camp/Dunford collaboration closes out the album on a relative high note.

The lyrics are nothing special. Haslam, singing well, and in the first person, tells of a desire (and a plan) to head for a place in the tropics, leaving the freezing Ukraine (land of 'the ice and snow … where the cold winds blow') behind. The vocal melody, like so many on this album, is similarly lacklustre – not bad enough to ruin the song, but not strong enough to enhance it.

The track does have its merits, however, most notably in its three major instrumental sections. The first of these is the introduction, which begins as a dramatic, very Russian-sounding piano and acoustic guitar duet (the piano part bears comparison to the opening of 'Kings and Queens', from the very first Renaissance album), before Camp's thick bass comes in to steer the piece toward the entrance of Haslam's vocal.

Even more interesting is the two-minute break in the middle, which begins as a drums and acoustic guitar duet. Camp's pounding, ominous-sounding bass then joins in, followed, ten seconds later, by a new drum pattern. Gosling adds a sprightly, cascading piano part shortly thereafter, and then follows it up with a tasteful synth line. At the conclusion of this episode, another one starts up, featuring a loud, arpeggiated acoustic guitar part, over which we get a highly distorted electric guitar solo – which, in turn, leads back into the conclusion of Haslam's vocal.

The final instrumental passage of interest is the outro, which begins with an acoustic guitar, this time strummed, rather than picked. After the band joins in (bass and drums, with a synthesizer lightly taking over the melody implied by the acoustic guitar's chord progression), we get another good electric guitar solo, before the track comes to its end on one final synthesized 'whoosh'.

Related Tracks

'Africa' 4:43 (Camp/Dunford)

Recorded in 1982, this modestly successful attempt at what has come to be called 'world music' saw its first release on *Da Capo*, a 1995 two-disc CD retrospective of Renaissance's career through 1983. It was also subsequently included on *Songs from Renaissance Days*.

It begins with the sound of African drumming, which is soon joined by singing – presumably from a field recording. Shortly thereafter Dunford's acoustic guitar and Camp's bass enter, laying the foundation over which Haslam then proceeds to sing. While the lyrics don't say much of interest about Africa, the melody is pleasant enough, and Haslam's vocal sounds great.

The track even takes a bit of a proggy turn in the middle, as the players first come almost to a complete stop, before re-entering with an exotic drum and bass duel. As this gradually intensifies, voices, and then synthesizer, enter the mix, creating a genuinely exciting soundscape (a rarity for Renaissance in this period), which Haslam then further intensifies by repeatedly singing, on top of this mix, the song's catchy chorus.

As one of the most inventive and interesting Renaissance tracks of the early 1980s period, and arguably one of the best, it is surprising that it was left in the can for thirteen years before finally being released.

'Writers Wronged' 4:00 (Camp/Dunford)

Like 'Africa', this was recorded in 1982, but not released until 1995, on *Da Capo*, and then also included on *Songs From Renaissance Days*.

Given the song's title and the fact that one of the band's most iconic songs, 'Mother Russia', is about Solzhenitsyn, one might assume that this one would also be about writers who are persecuted because of the political content of their work. And the first couple of verses, addressed in the second person to a writer who had endured 'years of struggle', and had 'sheltered the truth' before 'at last your voice was heard', support that interpretation.

But then the narration switches to the first person, as the singer speaks of 'dining at the country club', 'spending more time on the yacht', and 'wondering what to do now'. It is not clear how these two parts of the song's lyrics are connected to one another.

Musically the highlights are Camp's high-in-the-mix bass, Haslam's lead vocal, and a fine flute solo that immediately follows another highlight – Camp's very unusual playing at 1:40-1:54, where he doubles Haslam's vocal on his bass.

'America' 3:59 (Paul Simon)

A fine cover of Paul Simon's iconic song from the 1968 Simon & Garfunkel album, *Bookends*, this was recorded in the early 1980s, and frequently performed in the band's shows in that decade, before finally being released on *Songs From Renaissance Days*. Unlike Yes, who had radically lengthened and rearranged the song, so as to fit their progressive rock style, Renaissance's version is much more faithful to the original, relying on Haslam's lead vocal, and modest background accompaniment, to bring out the greatness already present in Simon's lyrics and tune. While some of the backing vocals sound a bit cheesy, this is a quibble. Given the decline in quality of the band's original material at this time, one wonders why they did not attempt more covers.

Time-Line (1983)

Personnel:
Jon Camp: bass, vocals, guitar
Michael Dunford: acoustic and electric guitars, backing vocals
Annie Haslam: vocals
Bimbo Adcock: saxophones
Peter Barron: drums
Peter Gosling: keyboards
Eddie Hardin: keyboards
Nick Magnus: keyboards
Ian Mosley: drums
Dave Thomson: trumpet
Producer: Renaissance
Release date: 1983
Highest chart position: 207 (US)
Running time of original LP: 41:39

Although *Camera Camera* turned out to be neither a critical nor a commercial success, the news was not all bad for Renaissance in 1981. The band undertook three American tours that year, and these were very well attended and well received. Having been left for dead by their previous record company, the group found it exciting to be back performing live in front of audiences again, and their many American fans were thrilled to have an opportunity to see them, as the departures of Tout and Sullivan, followed by the release of the Nevada singles, had made it seem that the band was finished.

Despite the fact that concert audiences responded much more positively to the old classics than to the newer synth-pop material, when Renaissance finally returned to the studio to record a follow up to *Camera Camera*, they chose to continue in the direction that album represented and made no effort to recapture their classic symphonic rock sound. With Thatcher having stopped writing for Renaissance, and Dunford clearly in a composing slump, this decision seems to have been the result of the band's main songwriting responsibilities now falling to Camp, who would go on to write all ten songs on the new album – four of them entirely on his own, and six in collaboration with Dunford, who confirms that Camp 'did the majority of the work' on the album. Upon its release, Camp publicly proclaimed *Time-Line* to be the band's best album, though he would later retract that claim.

'Flight' 4:06 (Camp/Dunford)
The album opener is an up-tempo, new wave style, rocker, with a few progressive flourishes. It starts off with an odd, stop-and-start, rhythm, in which three bars in 4/4 time are followed by one in 2/4 so that the downbeat of the fifth measure comes as something of a surprise. After four iterations of this

rhythm, the tempo slows down considerably, as an electric guitar solo leads us into the first vocal section, in which the pace picks up again.

Camp and Haslam share lead vocal duties, with Camp's voice more prominent in the first half of each verse, Haslam singing the second half alone, and Haslam also taking the lead on the choruses. They sing in the first person, and in character, as Camp plays the part of one who is saddened by his partner's departure on the 'flight' of the song's title ('I watched you fly away today/ You held me close and turned away/ And you were gone/ I said I couldn't understand/ Why you need a foreign land/ What's wrong with home?'), and Haslam plays the one who is leaving ('I need to breathe/ Need to see what this life's got in store for me/ Take a chance while I can').

At the conclusion of two verse/chorus alterations, there is a brief instrumental section, featuring solos on electric guitar and then synthesizer. A brief guitar and bass dialogue then leads us into another iteration of the chorus. This is followed by a brief episode in which a pattern of three short staccato blasts, followed by one longer one and a rest, is played six times, and then played in a slowed-down variation twice. This, in turn, leads to the song's concluding passage, a slowed-down, augmented variation on the chorus, ending with the words, 'I'm coming home/ I'm coming home/ I'm on a flight'.

Everything here works fairly well. It's easy to see why this track was selected to open the album.

'Missing Persons' 3:34 (Camp)

This short song, about the fear of 'disappearing' (whether literally or metaphorically) and being forgotten, suffers from the absence of a compelling melody, and from the 1980s-style heavily processed-sounding production.

'Chagrin Boulevard' 4:22 (Camp/Dunford)

As with the previous track, the problems here are too little melody and too much production. The lead vocals, shared by Haslam and Camp, are at times so buried behind electronic keyboard washes as to be rendered nearly inaudible. For example, the title of the song, 'Chagrin Boulevard', is mentioned in the chorus, but without knowledge of the title, and/or a lyric sheet, it is doubtful that a listener would know it. Both singers, but especially Camp, sometimes sound as if they are singing several hundred feet away from us, and away from the instrumentalists, who are very present.

Furthering the feeling of arbitrariness that pervades the song, it begins with an electric guitar solo that seems unconnected to the rest of the track.

'Richard IX' 3:38 (Camp)

Although this just a ditty, a weightless little pop song, it features an irresistibly catchy chorus. It is a pity that Haslam has to fight to be heard over the much too loud and busy background. The plastic, processed 1980s production sound also rankles.

'The Entertainer' 4:44 (Camp/Dunford)

The lyrics of this song are more interesting and meaningful than most in the post-Thatcher era, perhaps because in this case, they concern something that the band members undoubtedly understood very well and cared about deeply – the plight of the travelling entertainer. The song addresses the situation from several angles, including such issues as the rigours of travel, and the difficulty of performing up to expectations despite fatigue, boredom, or personal emotional obstacles ('Travel to places, fill all the spaces in everybody's lives/ Don't show the pressure, try not to measure how you feel inside'), as well as the problem of fans who think they have a personal relationship with the performers as people, simply on the basis of having an emotional connection to their work ('The entertainer's no stranger, she only lives to play/ The distance between us is only a note or two away').

While the vocal melodies, like most in the post-1978 period, are less than stellar, they are serviceable, in the sense that they don't stand as serious obstacles to the appreciation of the lyrics, or of the quality of Haslam's voice as she delivers them. And there are some musical delights to be found in this track. The song opens with a lovely, descending minor-key piano riff, which is rendered all the more enjoyable when Camp joins in with his initially melodic, then funky, bass accompaniment. When Haslam then enters with her lead vocal, the band accompanying her employs the same propulsive (BANG BANG soft soft) accent pattern that had been used so effectively on the opening track, 'Kings And Queens', of the very first Renaissance album, from the original, pre-Haslam, band, in 1969. And Haslam favours us with some impressive vocal acrobatics on the final line of the chorus: 'Music calls – come and see, come and see, come and see'. She raises the pitch on each iteration of 'come and see', such that the first 'see' lands on an A4 note, the second on a very high E5, and the third on a stratospheric A5. One of the great pleasures of listening to this track is getting to hear this climbing feat four times – twice as the chorus is first sung, then again when the chorus is repeated, and then once more as a stand-alone event, right at the end.

One problem with the track is worthy of note, however, since it is also found on several others on this album, and on some from the last couple of albums as well. The problem is that the beautiful timbre of Haslam's voice, which is readily apparent and easy to appreciate early in the track, gets increasingly buried in the mix as the song proceeds. One can still hear the words she is singing, and appreciate that she is hitting the notes, but the musical qualities of her voice are drowned out by the instrumental accompaniment. Why does this happen?

Perhaps the band is simply continuing with the Renaissance tradition of favouring arrangements in which there is a gradual build-up of instruments. In many Renaissance tunes from the band's classic period, Haslam would begin her lead vocal accompanied only by piano or acoustic guitar, with other instruments only coming in later, on the second verse, or on the chorus, and even then, often one at a time, rather than all at once. Such a technique mitigates the monotony of repeating the melodies of the verses and choruses because at least there is something new in the instrumental accompaniment. Moreover, since the change is one of addition, rather than subtraction, there is a sense of forward momentum, and of an increase in intensity. The obvious danger, however, is that the addition of instruments will result in the instrumental backing becoming louder, thus drowning out the vocal. Somehow the band was able to avoid this problem on its classic recordings and did so (usually) without resorting to the obvious and artificial-sounding device of simply lowering the volume of each instrument and/or jacking up that of Haslam's singing. Perhaps the key to this lies in the fact that almost all of the instruments in those recordings (piano, acoustic guitar, drums, and orchestral strings and brass) are acoustic instruments, which, in the hands of skilled players, can speak clearly, and make an impact, at moderate volume, without it sounding as if they are being muffled. The fact that Tout, Sullivan, and Dunford (when on acoustic guitar) were all very good at playing with restraint and at serving the song, rather than aggressively showing off, no doubt helps here. Additionally, the fact that their instruments were perhaps more compatible with the human voice than are the electronic keyboards and guitars of the band on the late 1970s and early 1980s Renaissance recordings is also significant. Thus handicapped by their instruments, and perhaps, in the case of some of the newer instrumentalists, not being as talented at the underappreciated art of playing as restrained accompanists, it could be that the drowning out of Haslam's vocal timbre is an unintended flaw in the arrangement and/or its execution.

But the other possibility is that the effect is deliberate. While Haslam's voice sounds gorgeous in the early part of this song (and of others), it also sounds somewhat out of place – a richly human element in a soundscape that otherwise sounds mechanical, electronic, and processed. But it is able to do so only to the degree that it stands out from, rather than blends in with, that artificial sounding background. So in this recording, as in others of this period, this problem of incongruity is solved by gradually raising the volume of the mechanical-sounding background to the point where Haslam's voice no longer stands out from it, but rather joins in with it, resulting in a track that is unified in its completely machine-like, highly processed sound, devoid of any human elements.

'Electric Avenue' 4:55 (Camp/Dunford)

A frustrating track, this one starts promisingly, with a surprisingly proggy instrumental introduction, before giving way to a bland, play-it-safe vocal melody that immediately dispenses with all of the delightful quirks that had made the introduction so intriguing.

The introduction also annoys, but only for a few seconds, as it begins with unpleasant electronic buzzing sounds. But Camp then enters with an aggressively twisted bassline, soon to be joined by some beautifully disjointed electric guitar work from Dunford, at which point we are almost in King

Crimson territory. At one minute in, the Camp/Dunford groove abruptly ceases, giving way to a short, fast, similarly Crimson-esque keyboard line. Camp responds to this, three seconds later, with an urgent, throbbingly repetitive, new bass part, over which, Haslam begins to sing.

She and Camp share the lead vocal, and both do the best they can with the song's mediocre melody.

Guest musician Bimbo Adcock plays a nice solo in the middle, and a few fills later in the track, on saxophone, an instrument rarely featured in Renaissance recordings.

'Majik' 3:09 (Camp/Dunford)

This short, modestly catchy number goes by quickly and is easy to enjoy. One does have to contend with occasional, and seemingly random, annoying keyboard noises; and Camp's vocal responses to Haslam's singing the word 'Majik' in the 'What is happening to me?' chorus (there are six such responses), are so faint as to be almost inaudible and are indecipherable without a lyric sheet. That appears to be intentional, but the reason for it is unclear.

'Distant Horizons' 3:56 (Camp)

All of the album's faults are on display here: a mediocre vocal melody, a noisy backing track that fights with Haslam's lead vocal, and lyrics that make little sense. (We are repeatedly told that 'Political intervention/ Is something we shouldn't mention', but we are never told why – is it just because it makes for a nice rhyme?) In addition, this track contains no extended instrumental sections and nothing of interest in terms of the song's structure.

'Orient Express' 3:54 (Camp)

Bass and brass are the stars of this one. In the instrumental introduction, Camp's bass, placed very high in the mix, creates a strong pulse, thumping on a single note, once per beat, as guest musician Dave Thomson plays the piece's opening riff on trumpet. Then, when Haslam comes in with her lead vocal, Camp abruptly drops the monotonous pulse part, choosing instead to accompany the eccentric melody that she sings with an aggressively adventurous counter-melody of his own. His playing remains high in the mix, and remarkable, throughout the vocal sections, and in the very brief transitions among verses and choruses; and Thomson's occasional trumpet flourishes are effective here as well.

The major disappointment of the track is the 90-second outro, in which the robotic, heavily processed drums, and frequent noisy electronic keyboard interjections, dominate the soundscape. Whereas Tout, the original keyboardist of the Haslam era, had initially concentrated on piano, and then gradually shifted his focus to the simulation of orchestral instruments on electronic keyboards, Gosling (and perhaps the other two keyboardists listed in this album's credits) seems to prefer to use his electronic keyboards for the purpose of making buzzes, whooshes, spacey science fiction sounds, and industrial noises.

One wonders whether the loss of Tout may have negatively affected the quality of the band's arrangements generally, and not merely in regard to the keyboard sounds employed. Camp had said of Tout, while he was still in the band, that his 'expertise is in the arranging side of things. He doesn't write much music, but we bring him ideas and he puts on the glossing, which because of his classical training, is much easier for him to do. It's very difficult to arrange a Renaissance song on guitar. It's a lot easier to do on piano'. This seems significant, in that the problem with most of the post-Tout era Renaissance songs is not that they are without good bits, but rather that the good bits aren't developed very far, are not connected up well with other good bits, and are conjoined with a lot of annoying bits that needn't be in the arrangement at all.

'Autotech' 5:21 (Camp/Dunford)

The longest track on the album, and the only one to crack the five-minute barrier, this up-tempo album closer features Camp on a low-in-the-mix lead vocal.

The piece begins with a protracted zoomy synthesizer episode, over which the band eventually comes in to play a noisy, edgy, new wave-style groove, to serve as the foundation for Camp's distant-sounding vocal. Haslam, even lower in the mix, harmonises with him on the chorus and middle-eight. They sing incoherent lyrics to a mediocre tune.

There is a synth-heavy instrumental break in the middle, though it does include a couple of brief piano passages.

The track, and the album, come to an end on a brief 'bop bop bop' episode of vocalise from Camp and Haslam.

Related Tracks

'You' 8:18 (Camp/Dunford/Haslam)

One of several tracks that the team of Camp, Dunford, and Haslam made after the release of *Time-Line*, presumably as part of an unsuccessful effort to make a follow-up to that album, this lengthy, modestly proggy piece was often featured in the band's live set in the 1980s before finally being released as a bonus studio track on an otherwise live album, 1997's *King Biscuit Flower Hour, Vol. Two* (also known as *Live at the Royal Albert Hall with the Royal Philharmonic Orchestra, Part Two*). It also appeared on *Songs From Renaissance Days*, released that same year.

On the *King Biscuit Flower Hour* album cover, the song is listed as having a 'Part 1' and a 'Part 2'. The entire song, as its title suggests, is sung in the second person singular, but in Part 1, Haslam sings to 'You' about the good things you have brought into her life, whereas in Part 2, this same 'You' has 'left me reeling', leaving a 'void around me', and thus should 'realise you were wrong', and 'feel the need for me'.

This division into two parts is also expressed musically, as Part 1 is played at a slow tempo, with Haslam singing over a background consisting primarily of arrhythmic keyboard washes, whereas Part 2 proceeds at a much quicker pace, over a driving, full band, rhythmic groove.

While Haslam takes the lead vocal for most of the song, there are two verses, in which Haslam sings the first two lines, and Camp, echoing her, takes the last two, with their voices briefly overlapping in counterpoint – a nice effect, and one of the track's musical highlights.

Further musical variety is provided by a moderately lengthy instrumental section, which attempts a few classic Renaissance-style twists and turns.

The main weakness of the track is its keyboard-dominated arrangement, as the keyboards are frequently too loud in the mix, and often emit irritating sounds that clash with the other instruments.

'Dreamaker' 4:59 (Camp/Dunford)

Another song from the band's 1980s setlist, and another post-*Time-Line* recording released on *Songs From Renaissance Days*, this one features lyrics, by Camp, about a teenage girl who longs to be a star, set to a lovely Dunford melody. On balance, the track succeeds, largely on the strength of its tune, and of Haslam's vocal performance in rendering it. A special highlight is the sound of Haslam harmonising with herself on the lines, 'She's only living for today/ Don't you take her breath away', in the chorus.

But on the negative side, the keyboard-heavy instrumental backing is both too loud and too shrill throughout the song, partially obscuring the delicate beauty of Dunford's melody. And, at the conclusion of the singing, the song ends on a shockingly repetitive (and consequently boring) outro, which lasts more than a minute.

Dunford and Haslam presumably both liked this melody, as they each subsequently re-recorded it in the 1990s. However, this song would bear a different title, 'Love Lies, Love Dies', in these newer recordings, as former Renaissance lyricist Betty Thatcher had by then written new words to Dunford's tune.

'Only When I Laugh' 4:10 (Camp/Dunford/Haslam)

Yet another post-*Time-Line* recording released on *Songs From Renaissance Days*, this one, like 'You', is a song about a broken relationship, sung in the second person to the absent former partner. Haslam's terrific lead vocal isn't enough to prop this one up, as Dunford's melody fails to catch fire (despite five iterations of its mediocre chorus), and the track is further marred by spectacularly monotonous drumming.

'The Body Machine' 4:08 (Camp/Dunford/Haslam)

A lightweight pop song with a catchy chorus, this is another post-*Time-Line* recording released on *Songs From Renaissance Days*. Here the 1980s-style keyboard and drum sounds are well suited to the material, as is Haslam's deliberately wide-eyed, naïve-sounding vocal. A fluffy, inconsequential, repetitive (the chorus is sung five times) little tune, it works, for what it is.

'No Beginning No End' 5:06 (Dunford/Betty Newsinger)

On this mid-1980s track, ultimately released on *Songs From Renaissance Days*, Dunford resumes his writing partnership with Renaissance's former chief lyricist Betty Thatcher, who had by this time changed her last name back to its original 'Newsinger', in an effort to distance herself from the politics of 1980s era British Prime Minister Margaret Thatcher.

Neither the lyrics nor the tune are memorable, and such good qualities as the track does possess, such as Haslam's fine vocal, are not helped by its bland, generic, 1980s-style drum and keyboards sounds, or its antiseptic 1980s-style production.

'Northern Lights' 4:24 (Dunford/Thatcher)

A pointless remake of the 1978 hit single, this mid-1980s version is included on *Songs From Renaissance Days*. The band attempts to give the song a 1980s sound and feel, mainly by deemphasising the acoustic guitar part, making the rhythm more square and monotonous (mostly by means of a hideous drum track), adding some cheesy keyboard sounds, and completely removing the delightful keyboard and bass baroque-style duet that had been a highlight of the original recording (on the 'Marking the space between the days/ Early hours pass away/ I sing to you of northern lights/ I sing for you of northern nights' part). Haslam's singing is fine, but even she, quite understandably, fails to match the level of energy and enthusiasm that she had achieved on the original recording.

Still, the song is so good that even these imperfections can only diminish it to a fairly small degree. So this is still a good recording – but a completely unnecessary one for those who have the original.

Tuscany (2000)

Personnel:
Michael Dunford: acoustic guitars, backing vocals
Annie Haslam: vocals
Mickey Simmonds: keyboards, backing vocals
Terence Sullivan: drums, percussion
Alex Caird: bass
Roy Wood: bass, keyboards, percussion, backing vocals
John Tout: piano, harpsichord, keyboards
Rob Williams: backing vocals
Producer: Michael Dunford, Annie Haslam, and (as co-producer of 'In the Sunshine') Roy Wood
Release date: 2000
Highest chart position: Did not chart
Running time of original CD: 49:23

Time-Line bombed, generating poor sales and the harshest reviews of any Renaissance album. All three members of the band that created it went on to disown it. Dunford, calling the album 'pretty awful', took the long view on the career of his band: 'Our music was a breath of fresh air and our only mistake was trying to change it. After *A Song for All Seasons*, I think we totally lost our way. *Azure D'Or* was just trying to jump on what was going on at the time, as were the following two albums *Camera Camera* and *Time-Line*'.

Haslam has repeatedly expressed similar views: 'We blew it with *Camera Camera* and *Time-Line*. We were unique in what we were doing, and we should have taken that format into the Eighties. It was a shame. It started a little bit with *Azure D'Or*, and then with *Time-Line* and *Camera Camera*, we sounded like everybody else. It didn't matter that my voice was still unique because I didn't have the vehicle or great songs to use. Personally, I feel we shouldn't have abandoned who we were and our heritage'.

Even Camp, who seems to have been the driving force within the band during their early 1980s change of direction, has since expressed dissatisfaction with *Camera Camera* and *Time-Line*: 'I was never happy with those albums.... Because we were no longer with a major label, we didn't have anywhere near as much money to spend on the albums.... I liked a couple of the tracks, but it was a little too poppy for my liking'.

Despite the spectacular failure of *Time-Line*, it appeared, at first, as though Renaissance would continue to thrive as a live act. Although Peter Gosling and Peter Barron, who had played on *Camera* and *Time-Line*, departed, a new ad in *Melody Maker* brought in fresh recruits in the form of drummer Gavin Harrison and keyboardist Mike Taylor; and the *Time-Line* tour, featuring the quintet of Camp, Dunford, Haslam, Harrison, and Taylor, showed that Renaissance could still sell concert tickets. Moreover, the new line-up started to work on new material, and recorded a few tracks, presumably as part of a new album project. However, Harrison and Taylor left after the 1983 tour, and then, not surprisingly, IRS, the label for which the band had made *Camera* and *Time-Line*, dropped them the next year.

In spite of these setbacks, Camp, Dunford, and Haslam tried valiantly to keep Renaissance alive, even going so far as to perform acoustic sets as a three-piece band. As Camp recalls it, 'We'd be coming to America, we were playing clubs, as a three-piece: Annie, Micky, and myself. Now, Renaissance does not work as a three-piece. It needs keyboards, it needs percussion, and it was like ... We were becoming an English version of Peter, Paul, and Mary, and that wasn't me'. Eventually, the trio brought in Greg Carter on drums and Raphael Rudd on keyboards and continued to tour into 1985, before Camp finally decided that it was time to leave.

The band then replaced Camp with Mark Lampariello (also known as 'Mark Lambert'), and Carter with percussionist Charles Descarfino, with whom Dunford, Haslam, and Rudd continued to tour, but now as an acoustic quintet, into 1987. However, as Dunford explains, in order for the band to remain viable it 'needed a new album to promote, and we couldn't get one together, so we decided to call it a day'. The once-mighty Renaissance thus played what appeared at the time to be its final gig, in a small club in a small city, Sayreville, New Jersey, on 6 June 1987, before disbanding.

This remained the situation through most of the 1990s, although both Haslam and Dunford, each in a half-hearted way, would invoke the Renaissance name during this period in connection with solo projects, with Haslam releasing an album under the name 'Annie Haslam's Renaissance,' and Dunford responding with two albums by 'Michael Dunford's Renaissance'. (These albums are discussed in a separate chapter on solo albums and related recordings.)

But in the late 1990s, Haslam and Dunford decided to join forces once again and to make a more serious effort at reuniting the classic Renaissance line-up. Toward that end they managed to bring Terry Sullivan and John Tout back into the fold to work with them on a new album project, which would then be missing only one member of the 1972-1979 line-up, Jon Camp. The original plan was for this quartet to make the album, with Roy Wood filling in on bass, as a guest musician. However, the recording of the album ended up requiring two sessions, and Tout and Wood, because of prior commitments, were unable to participate in the second. So Mickey Simmonds, on keyboards, and Alex Caird, on bass, were recruited to help complete the album.

With lyricist Haslam and composer Dunford collaborating on all ten of the album's tracks, the band abandoned the synth-pop style they had adopted in the 1980s and tried to return to their classic 1970s sound.

'Lady from Tuscany' 6:40 (Haslam/Dunford)

Just a few seconds into this album opener Haslam begins to sing wordlessly and continues to do so for the better part of a minute, thus showing off the power, range, and beautiful timbre of her voice. At the conclusion of this vocalise episode the band kicks in, and, with Dunford's acoustic guitar, Sullivan's drums, and guest musician Alex Caird's bass, the classic Renaissance sound is mostly recaptured. The main ingredient missing is Tout's piano, but at least Mickey Simmonds uses his electronic keyboards for classical style orchestration, rather than spacey whooshes, buzzes, and gurgles, or the creation of robotic dance rhythms.

Haslam's lyrics, about a great violinist's affair with a 'lady from Tuscany', are set to a decent, but not outstanding, Dunford melody, beautifully conveyed by Haslam's vocal.

In the outro, she returns for another performance of vocalise, this time sounding distant, as the atmospheric track comes to a close.

Judging by this opening piece, the new incarnation of Renaissance would seem to be operating at some distance from the standard of 'Ashes Are Burning', 'Mother Russia', or 'Song of Scheherazade'. Happily, they appear to be in a place even further away from anything on *Camera Camera* or *Time-Line*.

'Pearls Of Wisdom' 4:25 (Haslam/Dunford)
With the addition of Tout's piano, the lead instrument on this track, the band comes even closer to recapturing the classic Renaissance sound than it had done on 'Lady from Tuscany'. Dynamic contrast is used effectively here, as the piece builds from a first half in which Haslam sings over a quiet, piano-and-acoustic-guitar-based, accompaniment, to a climactic 'Oh as the love flows' conclusion, featuring the entire band, keyboard orchestration, and a chorus of background singers (Haslam and Simmonds, multi-tracked), all letting it rip. The melody, while far from Dunford's best, is pretty good, and Haslam and the band elevate it with their strong performance.

'Eva's Pond' 3:40 (Haslam/Dunford)
In this piece, the only instrumentalist supporting Haslam's vocal is Simmonds, on keyboards. While it is never unpleasant to hear Haslam sing, here neither the lyrics (a fairly straightforward narrative about falling in love amidst the beauties of nature), nor the melody, nor the accompaniment rises above the ordinary.

'Dear Landseer' 5:19 (Haslam/Dunford)
The 'Landseer' of the title is Edwin Landseer, the nineteenth-century English artist, noted for his paintings of animals ('You paint a dog, a stag, a hawk, a deer'), and for his lion sculptures at the base of Nelson's Column in Trafalgar Square. Haslam's lyrics are in the form of a letter to Landseer, thanking him for the painting he had made for Queen Victoria to cheer her up after the death of her husband.

The track starts with simple instrumentation, as both the instrumental introduction and the initial accompaniment to Haslam's vocal feature acoustic guitar and little else. But then, as in the case of 'Pearls of Wisdom', the instrumental backing intensifies and becomes more complex, as the full band joins in to support Haslam's rendering of Dunford's good, but not great, melody.

A highlight of the piece is a brief vocalise episode, in the middle of the track, in which Haslam sings vowel sounds gloriously.

If one were to offer quibbles, they might be that the otherwise fine orchestration is a bit too noticeably a keyboard simulation and that the otherwise fine outro is overly repetitious.

'In The Sunshine' 4:25 (Haslam/Dunford)

Although this song is about a loved one who is now dead and gone, both the music and the lyrics ('And though we're far apart/ We'll always have our love/ We'll always be the same') put a happy spin on this sad situation. The dense faux orchestral instrumentation tries to make a major statement out of a rather slight tune. With a few exceptions, most notably 'Northern Lights', Renaissance tends to do dark and moody better than light and happy.

'In My Life' 5:26 (Haslam/Dunford)

In this poignant song, Haslam sings, over a suitably restrained accompaniment (mostly piano, acoustic guitar, and very light percussion) of regret over a failed relationship. She also sings of a desire to rekindle the affair ('I would turn back the clock today/ I'd be faithful and true/ We could be in love again/ There's nothing that I wouldn't do/ To have you in my life'), but does so in such a way as to suggest both a desperate hope, and a resigned recognition that the hope will not be fulfilled. It is a skilful and affecting vocal performance.

The melody, while still falling well short of Dunford's mid-1970s standard, is good enough to make the track thoroughly enjoyable.

'The Race' 4:58 (Haslam/Dunford)

The one track on the album that is uncomfortably reminiscent of the band's 1980s synth-pop output, this up-tempo tune about an athlete's love of competing, winning, and receiving the crowd's adulation, is sung over a background of jittery keyboards, a loud, plodding bass line, and robotically metronomic drumming. At least the production is clean, avoiding the antiseptic feeling of many of the band's 1980s tracks. Dunford's melody is not particularly memorable.

'Dolphin's Prayer' 3:19 (Haslam/Dunford)

This song expresses love and concern for dolphins, highly intelligent and friendly animals that are sometimes accidentally beached on seashores. One can agree with this sentiment, and also acknowledge that the topic might be a suitable one for a good song – but, alas, this one falls short.

The piece has a very simple construction. Haslam sings the lyrics straight through, occasionally harmonising with herself, accompanied almost exclusively by a slow-moving keyboard part. Neither the melody, nor the lyrics, nor the accompaniment are quite compelling enough to command or sustain interest.

'Life In Brazil' 3:40 (Haslam/Dunford)

In this cheerful, up-tempo tribute to Brazil, the best moments are those in which the band, always just in brief flashes, experiments with Latin rhythms, especially on piano and percussion instruments. Otherwise, the lyrics and tune are both rather bland – perhaps simply another instance of the band not being in its element when going for a light and happy vibe.

'One Thousand Roses' 7:12 (Haslam/Dunford)

In keeping with Renaissance tradition, this album closer is also the album's longest track. Moreover, it is the one that comes closest to emulating the band's 1970s-style multi-section epics, although here there are only three major sections: a slow, stately melody at the beginning and end; a brisk, rocking romp in between; and a synth-heavy instrumental interlude between the up-tempo middle and the leisurely-paced ending. The rocking middle section is by far the most engaging of the three, followed by the instrumental break, which only suffers from its timbral inconsistency with the rest of the track. But the meandering, unmemorable quality of the melody at the beginning and the end drags the piece down a bit.

'One Thousand Roses' thus stands as a microcosm of the *Tuscany* album as a whole – good enough to make one glad to have it, to make one happy that the Renaissance band is alive again, to stand as an improvement over the 1980s albums, and to give one hope that future delights might yet be forthcoming; but disappointing in that there has been no return either to the melodic standard, level of structural complexity, or ambitiousness in terms of scale, that had characterised the band's music, and made it so special, in the 1972-1978 period.

Grandine il Vento (2013)/Symphony Of Light (2014)

Personnel:
Tom Brislin: keyboards & backing vocals
Michael Dunford: acoustic guitars, backing vocals
Jason Hart: keyboards, accordion, backing vocals
Annie Haslam: vocals
David J. Keyes: bass, double bass, vocals
Frank Pagano: drums, percussion, backing vocals
Rave Tesar: keyboards, piano
Ian Anderson: flute on 'Cry to the World'
John Wetton: vocal on 'Blood Silver Like Moonlight'
Producer: Annie Haslam and Rave Tesar
Release date: 2013 (*Grandine il Vento*)/April 2014 (*Symphony Of Light*)
Highest chart position: Did not chart
Running time of original CD: 54:16 (*Grandine il Vento*)/67:47 (*Symphony Of Light*)
Note: The Japanese release of *Grandine il Vento* contains a live recording of 'Carpet of the Sun' as a bonus track. This is discussed in a separate chapter on the band's live recordings.

To promote *Tuscany,* the new Renaissance line-up (the album band of Dunford, Haslam, Simmonds, and Sullivan, plus two long-time members of Haslam's group, keyboardist Rave Tesar and bassist David J. Keyes) gave a concert at the 2,000-seat London Astoria, followed by a three-gig mini-tour of Japan. A double-CD live album, from one of the performances in Japan, was released in 2002. (It is discussed in a separate chapter on the band's live recordings). But in October of that year, Haslam released a statement that Renaissance was, once again, disbanding.

This decision apparently resulted from several factors – the sales of *Tuscany,* and of the follow-up live album, had been disappointing; Dunford, from the beginning, had been reluctant to sign on for more than one album; and the group discovered that concert promoters were not willing to offer terms that would make a European tour as a six-piece outfit economically viable.

But in fall 2009 Haslam and Dunford decided to give the band one more shot, putting together a new version of Renaissance for a nine-city tour of the US (focused primarily on the east coast) in celebration of the group's 40th anniversary. Haslam later commented that she and Dunford 'decided that we wanted to go back to what we did the best, which was symphonic rock, and not try to follow any new trends of the time, because that is what made us unique'.

The line-up for the tour consisted of Dunford and Haslam, Tesar and Keyes from the 2001-2002 configuration, and two new recruits, keyboardist Tom Brislin and drummer Frank Pagano. The tour was successful, and the strength of the interest in the new Renaissance motivated the band to do some recording. First came a 2010 EP, *The Mystic And The Muse*, a collection of three new original songs. Then, in the following year, with Jason Hart replacing Brislin at one of the group's two keyboard slots, came a 2 CD/1 DVD live set, in which the *Turn Of The Cards* and *Scheherazade And Other Stories* albums, plus the title track from the recent EP, were performed in their entirety. (It, too, is discussed in the chapter on the band's live recordings.)

Next on the agenda was the idea of making a new full-length studio album. However, the band realized that this could only happen if they financed it, upfront, themselves. So they set up a Kickstarter page, reluctantly asking their fans to invest in the project, which would cost an estimated $44,000. The fans came through in spectacular fashion, pledging more than double that amount, a total exceeding $92,000. So the album, *Grandine il Vento*, was indeed made and released by the band in 2013. The following year Renaissance was able to obtain a distribution deal for it, provided that it could be sold under a different name, and with the inclusion of additional tracks. Thus, the album was re-released in 2014 under the title, *Symphony Of Light*, with the inclusion of three songs that had not been on *Grandine il Vento*. Two of these were tracks from *The Mystic And The Muse*, the band's 2010 EP (the song 'The Mystic and the Muse', first recorded for that EP, had already appeared on *Grandine il Vento*), with the third being a new song, written and recorded specifically for *Symphony Of Light*.

Sadly, two significant deaths occurred during this period. Betty Thatcher (later Betty Newsinger), the band's chief 1970s-era lyricist, died on 15 August 2011. Then, on 20 November 2012, shortly after completing his work on *Grandine Il Vento*, Michael Dunford died, unexpectedly, at his home, from a cerebral haemorrhage. When Renaissance toured in 2013 in support of *Grandine Il Vento*, the guitarist slot was filled by Ryche Chlanda.

'Symphony Of Light' 12:09 (Haslam/Dunford)
Whereas on *Tuscany* Renaissance had attempted to recapture the *sound* of its classic mid-70s recordings, with this opening track the band finally, for the first time since 1978, tries also to revive something of the *style* of its work from that period, for this is, indeed, a proggy, classically-influenced, multi-section epic. Something on that scale would seem to be required in order to match the grandeur of the song's subject matter – the great genius and polymath of the Italian Renaissance (and thus an appropriate topic for the band, Renaissance!), the painter, scientist, and inventor, Leonardo da Vinci.

The production is extraordinarily clean, spacious, and uncluttered, allowing every element of the recording to be heard clearly. While Haslam's voice had, quite understandably, changed a bit in the thirteen years that had passed since the release of *Tuscany*, with a slight, but noticeable, decrease in power, suppleness, and fullness of tone, she nonetheless sings very well here, and still sounds great – expressive, with a bell-like tone, a warm vibrato (not something that she had often employed in the past), and a wide range, as she maintains her tone, and conveys no sense of straining, even while singing notes that are extremely far apart from one another. For example, at just after three minutes, she goes down to hit an F#3 (a note that she had visited several times in this section), only to leap up to a stratospheric A5 just three seconds later. The seven-note descending vocalise melody that she sings there, and twice repeats, is one of the highlights of the track. There is great inventiveness in her singing, right from the outset, as evidenced by the little swooping crescendo she applies to her first note, and then her 'yodelled' grace note on the word 'light.'

Fun and interesting instrumental sections abound. Examples include the church bells/synthesizer/acoustic guitar passage, that introduces the 'No man here on earth' vocal section; the rocking faux horns passage at 4:19, which gives way to a gentle acoustic guitar/piano/bass response; the brief piano solo at 6:54; the lovely piano and bass duet at 7:15 – one of several quiet passages in the track; the short organ and drum blast at 7:45; then, perhaps most enjoyable of all, the riffy bass/synthesizer/percussion/acoustic guitar episode that begins at 7:51; and, finally, the passage commencing at 9:44, in which we first hear a hectic, descending piano line, followed by a part in which a piano imitates a harp, and does so while swimming among ominous faux-strings chords played on an electronic keyboard.

A notable advantage of a lengthy piece like this is that it allows for a more effective use of repetition than is possible in a song of more typical rock song length. For in the latter case, melodies return before one has had a chance to miss them. But in this track, some of the instrumental passages just described, and vocal sections as well, repeat, but only after they have been absent for a while so that their return is like a welcome reunion with a long-absent friend.

In 1995 Dunford had remarked that times had changed, making it no longer feasible to do songs that are 'too involved', or that last over six minutes, since 'the attention span can't take it anymore'. Given the length (over twelve minutes) and complexity of this outstanding track, one can be thankful that he must either have changed his mind or else decided that the times had changed again.

'Waterfall' 4:44 (Haslam/Dunford)

A track that both begins and ends with rainforest sounds, this is clearly a showcase for Haslam's impressive vocal, as there are no extended instrumental sections, and the accompaniment to her high-in-the-mix singing is extremely restrained – for the most part, just gentle acoustic guitar, very light percussion, and a bit of one-note-at-a-time piano.

Since the vocal melody is merely serviceable, listening to this piece makes for a mildly pleasant experience, but not a moving or memorable one.

'Grandine il Vento' 6:29 (Haslam/Dunford)

Another Haslam vocal showcase, this one is built on the contrast between the bland, sparsely accompanied verses, and the exciting, catchy, full-band-accompanied choruses and outro. The piece ends with Haslam, on top of a rocking, fully engaged band, triumphantly blasting an A5 note, and then holding it for ten seconds, as the band responds with four final, spaced-out D minor chords – in a manner reminiscent of the band's ending to live performances of 'Ashes Are Burning'.

'Porcelain' 6:41 (Haslam/Dunford)

Though this is, harmonically, perhaps the simplest song in the entire Renaissance catalogue, somehow it works.

Hand drums, keyboards, and a mallet instrument (perhaps marimba) set the stage for the singing of the first verse. But the magic of the piece is the oft-repeated chorus, which consists, for the most part, of a simple three-chord progression sung by Haslam and the band's several backing singers, in 'Aaahh, Aaahh, Aaahh' vocalise.

This same progression completely takes over the last third of the song at, as it is either played or implied, over and over again, for the entire remaining two minutes of the track, encompassing an instrumental interlude, a spoken-word final verse, a final iteration of the chorus, and an outro. Inexplicably, this repetitive pattern does not wear out its welcome, remaining a modest treat to the very end.

'Cry To The World' 5:44 (Haslam/Dunford)

The most distinctive feature of this track is the flute playing of guest musician Ian Anderson, the famous composer/flautist/guitarist/singer/frontman for the legendary band, Jethro Tull. Haslam explains how this happened:

> When we wrote this song, it was obvious that we really needed a flute in there and so, when we did the demos, we did a flute sound. Then, I said: 'I'm going to contact Ian Anderson and ask him if he wants to do it'. I contacted him and he said, 'I'm on tour in Eastern Europe but if you want to send me a WAV file of the song I will do something on my day off in my hotel room and see how it comes out. And if it's good enough, you can use it'. And he sent it back and it was perfect. Rave and I were giggling with excitement when we heard it. We both went, 'Oh my God!' We were just so excited.

Anderson solos briefly in the middle of the track, and again in the outro, but also provides several nice fills during the vocal sections. There is great variety in his playing, as it includes both aggressive, guttural, flutter tonguing passages, other passages in which he employs a pure, clean tone, and still others in which he effortlessly goes back and forth between the two techniques.

While the piece is definitely elevated by his playing, it otherwise suffers from an undistinguished vocal melody. The result is an interesting and moderately enjoyable track, but not one of the album's highlights.

'Air Of Drama' 5:20 (Haslam/Dunford)

On this track, melodically stronger than most of Dunford's post-1970s work,

Haslam duets with bassist David J. Keyes, whose relaxed, confident vocal sits well alongside Haslam's own.

While the piece is somewhat repetitious, with multiple iterations of the verse and chorus melodies, it is very effectively arranged, as variety is provided through shifts in the accompaniment. While maintaining a chamber music feel throughout, the dominant instrument backing the singers changes frequently (by turns, harpsichord, faux flute, accordion, faux strings, and piano), without the changes ever sounding forced or showy.

Perhaps the highlight of the track is a brief episode in which Haslam and Keyes take a break from the verses and choruses and instead sing vocalise 'ah's, before yielding to a dramatic instrumental passage in which a keyboard, imitating a plucked cello, plays an intense melody, which is periodically interrupted by brief, crashing, full-band chords.

'Blood Silver Like Moonlight' 5:15 (Haslam/Dunford)

Another track with a lovely, moody, melody, this one features guest John Wetton, the highly regarded veteran of such bands as King Crimson, UK, and Asia, here joining Haslam in a vocal duet, accompanied solely by piano. Their voices complement each other well in this varied vocal arrangement, in which they sometimes sing alone, taking turns, at other times sing together in unison, an octave apart, and finally, at the end, sing counterpoint melodies on top of one another.

Rave Tesar's piano solo is also noteworthy, as is his playing in the introduction and in accompaniment to the singing.

'The Mystic And The Muse' 7:51 (Haslam/Dunford)

Like 'Symphony of Light', this is a complex, proggy track, that harkens back to the band's mid-1970s glory years. It is a dark piece, with twists and turns enough to fill a track double its length.

It begins with an edgy, insistent, electronic keyboard lick, doubled on piano and faraway voice (perhaps a keyboard patch), that takes on an even more ominous tone when it is joined by Keyes' countermelody on bass. A brief, cascading piano line, entering simultaneously with drums, complicates matters further, as bombastic, threatening chords, played on piano and faux strings, suddenly rain down on us, punctuated by occasional drum fills. Next comes a flowing, rippling piano passage, accompanied now by scary organ chords. Then Haslam joins in, adding a high-pitched vocalise part that further ratchets up the track's atmosphere of menace.

This suddenly gives way to a rapid, descending line played on a mallet instrument, which in turn spills into a bass and hand drums episode, with other percussion instruments soon joining in, including, the return of the mallet instrument.

The playing comes to a complete stop only to resume again, with loud electronic keyboard chords now being laid on top of the on-going bass/hand drums/percussion/mallet instrument episode, which has since been joined by Dunford's strummed acoustic guitar.

The sudden insertion of two quick chords then brings this passage to an abrupt stop. Two seconds later the track starts up again, with a Haslam vocalise line (less threatening than the one heard previously) over an intense full-band-plus-faux-orchestra accompaniment. The playing then stops again, resuming a second later for an eight-second-long bass, hand drums, percussion, and acoustic guitar episode, before stopping again. After another one-second pause, the track returns with a gong strike, which then leads to a slow succession of moderately ominous chords, played on faux string keyboards as well as organ. This episode, too, comes to a stop, with the track resuming one second later, on a repeating descending piano line against a faux strings background.

It is on top of this pattern that Haslam finally enters, to deliver the song's lyrics.

She yields for a faux orchestral instrumental break, which starts quietly, then becomes quite loud, and then, with the entrance of Dunford's acoustic guitar, becomes quiet again. Against the acoustic guitar/faux strings/light percussion background that the players establish, Haslam returns, to continue her vocal.

The track then takes another dramatic turn, as Haslam yields once again, this time to an up-tempo, high intensity, full volume, faux orchestral instrumental section. But this lasts only 28 seconds, after which the players suddenly calm down, and resume playing more restrained accompaniment parts, thus allowing Haslam to return to the task of singing (and now completing) the lyrics. After she has done so, the track ends on a final, dramatic and triumphant, bit of Haslam's patented high-pitched vocalise.

'Tonight' 4:25 (Haslam/Dunford)
A Haslam vocal showcase, this song, originally released on the 2010 EP, *The Mystic And The Muse*, suffers from a sub-par Dunford melody, and from lyrics, on the joy of love, that fail to say anything new.

'Immortal Beloved' 5:39 (Haslam/Dunford)
Another track from *The Mystic And The Muse* EP, this one features a catchy melody and a stirring vocal performance from Haslam. The outro, featuring Haslam and at least one of the band's male backup singers performing vocalise 'ah's, is a bit repetitious. Otherwise, this is a thoroughly enjoyable piece.

'Renaissance Man' 3:27 (Haslam/Rave Tesar)
The one new song written and recorded for *Symphony Of Light*, this is a tribute to Michael Dunford, who had died shortly after finishing his work on *Grandine il Vento*. Haslam has pointed out in interviews that ending the album with this track brings to the album a certain symmetry, in that its opening song, 'Symphony of Light', is about Leonardo da Vinci, the quintessential

'Renaissance man', and now the album ends with a song about Michael Dunford, who was also, in a different sense, a 'Renaissance man'.

Haslam's lyrics pay touching tribute to her beloved friend and bandmate. Sadly, Rave Tesar's meandering melody is not of the same calibre. Still, 'Renaissance Man' ends the album on a bittersweet note – which is entirely fitting for this band that does 'dark' so very sweetly.

To date (2021) *Symphony Of Light* is Renaissance's last studio album, and, with the death of principal composer Dunford, it is uncertain that there will be another. Should it indeed turn out to be the last album, the band will have gone out on a high note, as this album, featuring two lengthy, 1970s-style, proggy classics ('Symphony of Light' and 'The Mystic and the Muse') as well as several other good songs, is arguably the group's best one since 1978's *A Song For All Seasons* – eclipsing the two 1980s synth-pop albums (*Camera Camera* and *Time-Line*), the first comeback album of this century (*Tuscany*), and even 1979's *Azure d'Or*.

In any case, since reforming in 2009, Renaissance has remained active as a live concert band. The group has performed concerts every year since then, having appeared in the United States, Japan, South Korea, England, Belgium, Germany, Holland, Israel, Portugal, and Brazil. They are scheduled to play in Germany and Brazil in 2021. According to Haslam, 'There's still a place for us because we've stayed true to the core of the music. We faltered a bit in the 80s when we went completely in the wrong direction, but we came back'.

Some of the band's recent concert performances have been documented in two albums that have appeared since *Symphony Of Light*: *Live At The Union Chapel* (released in 2015 in DVD and digital audio formats) and *A Symphonic Journey: Live In Concert* (a 2 CD/1 DVD set, released in 2018). These are discussed in a separate chapter on the band's live releases.

Finally, one more significant death in the Renaissance family should be noted. John Tout, keyboardist, and pillar of the band's sound during its classic 1970s period, passed away on 1 May 2015.

Live Recordings – Audio And Video

Quite a large number of Renaissance live recordings have been released over the years, both in audio and video formats. Moreover, in addition to stand-alone live albums, several concert performances have been included as bonus tracks on studio album re-releases. This chapter discusses these live recordings in chronological order, based on the dates of the performances, rather than on the dates of release.

Past Orbits Of Dust (CD)
A 2012 release, this album collects eight live performances by the original Renaissance line-up (Cennamo, Hawken, McCarty, and Jane and Keith Relf), recorded at seven different venues in 1969 and 1970. (One studio outtake is also included.) As might be expected, the performances are a bit looser, and with more improvisation, than those on the studio albums. The sound quality is inconsistent from track to track, but, considering the era, and the fact that these performances were probably not professionally recorded for the purpose of eventual release, the quality is good, and the tracks are certainly listenable.

Live Fillmore West 1970 (also released as Live + Direct) (CD)
This CD includes a complete set that the original Renaissance line-up played at the famous Fillmore West in San Francisco on 6 March 1970. Because Renaissance was a support act that night, their set barely exceeded 35 minutes in length and consisted of only four songs. One of those four, 'No Name Raga', duplicates a track on *Past Orbits Of Dust*, as the version of this song on that CD is this very performance from the Fillmore. The other three also duplicate songs on *Past Orbits Of Dust*, but in different performances. These different versions, and the sound quality of the recordings of them, are similar to one another, except that the performance of 'Bullet' at the Fillmore is truncated, being more than three minutes shorter than the studio version, and barely over half the length of the one on *Past Orbits of Dust*.

To supplement this short concert recording, the CD also includes four bonus studio tracks, and one of these, 'Statues', is also a *Past Orbits of Dust* duplicate. The other three, like 'Statues', are discussed under the 'Related Tracks' heading in connection with *Illusion*.

Kings And Queens (DVD)
A 2010 release, this DVD features two performances by the original Renaissance, from a 1970 German television broadcast, and five by the post-*Illusion* transitional line-up of Crowe, Cullom, Dunford, Korner, Slade, and Tout, filmed for a 1970 Belgian television show. The footage is significant historically, in that it constitutes the only good quality video documentation of the first incarnation of the band, and the only record of any kind for the transitional line-up, which never released any audio recordings.

DeLane Lea Studios 1973 (CD)

A 2015 release, this CD captures a live concert performed, with an audience, for a national radio broadcast, at the studio where Renaissance had recorded both *Prologue* and *Ashes Are Burning*. Here the classic 1970s Renaissance line-up (Camp, Dunford, Haslam, Sullivan, and Tout) performs seven songs, two from *Prologue* ('Sounds of the Sea' and the title song) and five of the six songs (omitting only 'On the Frontier') from the band's then-current album, *Ashes Are Burning*.

Andy Powell, of Wishbone Ash, and Al Stewart, the famed singer of 'Year of the Cat', appear as guests on 'Ashes Are Burning', with Powell performing a wilder, more frenetic, guitar solo than he had done on the studio track, and Stewart joining in with a backing vocal.

The sound quality is just fair – a bit tinny in spots, and with some audible tape hiss, but still quite listenable.

Ashes Are Burning (2019 Esoteric label reissue) (CD)

In January 1974 Renaissance recorded a three-song set for the BBC Radio One *In Concert* series. Their roughly 29-minute performance is included on this 2019 reissue of *Ashes Are Burning*. The three songs they perform, 'Can You Understand', 'Let It Grow', and 'Ashes Are Burning', are all drawn from that album, which was at the time the band's most recent release. The sound quality for the recording is very good throughout.

Academy Of Music 1974 (CD) and Turn Of The Cards (2020 Esoteric label reissue) (CD)

This 17 May 1974 concert at New York City's Academy of Music, which was originally simulcast on WNEW radio, has now been released twice on CD, first, in 2015, as a two-disc set, and then, in 2020, as discs two and three of a four-disc reissue of *Turn Of The Cards*.

Performing in support of the just-released *Turn Of The Cards*, the band here plays with an orchestra – the first time it had done so in a live performance. Andy Powell once again guests on 'Ashes Are Burning.'

The sound quality, while not perfect (for example, there are a few brief intrusions of feedback), is good, with the *Turn Of The Cards* 2020 reissue production standing as a slight improvement (but only that) over the previously released stand-alone version. Another difference between the two is that the 2020 production is about eleven minutes shorter, as it edits out most of Camp's stage announcements and commentary, as well as a great deal of audience applause.

Live At Carnegie Hall (LP, CD)

The most important live album in the band's catalogue, this two-LP set, released in 1976, was recorded at three concerts, on 20, 21, and 22 June 1975, at New York City's Carnegie Hall, with the New York Philharmonic Orchestra. It is the only live album that the band released during its classic 1972-1978 period, and it made an impact, charting at number 55 in the US, staying on the charts for 20 weeks, and receiving widespread critical acclaim. It is extremely well recorded, with excellent sound quality, especially by the standards of live recordings of this period. The very difficult task of achieving a good balance between band and orchestra is successfully pulled off here, one of the factors making this a more satisfying recording than the otherwise excellent *Academy of Music* concert. The players seemed to be in especially good spirits during these concerts, proud of the fact that they were headlining at such a prestigious venue, even more proud of the fact that they had sold it out for three consecutive nights (the first British band to do so), excited to be performing with a 30-piece orchestra, and buoyed by the response they received from the enthusiastic audiences.

By far the most controversial track on the album is the encore, an extended version, lasting over 22 minutes, of 'Ashes Are Burning'. The extra length is due to the inclusion of extended solos by Tout and Camp in the song's middle section, as well as a greatly expanded coda. Of all Renaissance recordings, this is probably the one that is most often criticised for allegedly indulging in the excesses that are said to typify the progressive rock genre. For example, a recent historian of 1970s-era British progressive rock complains that Camp's lengthy bass solo is only 'superficially impressive', and that 'typical of the era', it 'goes on for far too long without really adding anything to the song'. And, without going anywhere near that far, Haslam is quoted, in the liner notes to the 2019 reissue, as saying, 'I don't believe we should have done 'Ashes Are Burning'. It was too long...and had too many solos in it. Looking back, I'd love to have replaced it with something else'.

This would be my counterargument. First, since Renaissance, when playing live, generally performs fairly faithful reproductions of the original studio versions of its songs, and avoids lengthy solos, it adds variety to the concert to have one song that deviates from this standard practice. Moreover, the solos are outstanding, and they do also 'add something to the song', in the form of delayed gratification. In this version, the song's climactic section, Haslam's stunningly soft, beautiful, emotive, pitch-perfect rendering of the 'Imagine the burning embers' verse, does not arrive until 15:34, with the absolute climax, her spine-tingling, hair-raising, major ninth leap (accompanied by a dynamic leap of similar magnitude) on the line, 'Ashes are burning the WAAAAAAYYYYY!', not arriving until over a minute later. The extra time, compared to the studio recording, conveys the sense that one has travelled a longer distance to get there, thus making the payoff more intense – a conclusion that is consistent with the very audible audience reaction to this special moment.

Finally, with no electric guitarist on hand to duplicate Andy Powell's solo, Haslam then steps in, as she had done in the January 1974 BBC Radio One concert, to provide, as part of a six-minutes-plus coda, a series of high-pitched vocalise riffs, in which she comfortably reaches B5 notes several times before leaping up to a preposterous E6, and then hitting it twice more. One is in no hurry to have these spectacular riffs come to an end. In addition to their abundant musical merits, taken on their own, they also, in the context of what had immediately preceded them, give the listener a chance to recover at some leisure from the intensity of the climax, rather than have that experience too abruptly end in silence. (And the actual ending, featuring four triumphant gong strikes, is thrilling as well.)

The 2019 Esoteric label reissue restores a fine rendition of 'Kiev' to the program. (It had been performed at the concerts, but cut, for reasons of time restrictions, from the original LP version.) This package also contains, as a bonus CD, a 25 March 1976 London performance that had been recorded for another BBC Radio One *In Concert* program. This five-song, non-orchestral, hour-long program repeats songs from the Carnegie Hall setlist. The sound quality is very good.

British Tour '76 (CD)

A 2006 release, this is a recording of a 24 January 1976 Nottingham concert, part of a tour in support of *Scheherazade and Other Stories*. Recorded just 7 months after the Carnegie Hall concerts, all six of its songs duplicate offerings on that live album.

Once again, the performances are excellent (though there is no orchestra), and the sound quality of the recording is good, though not equal to the standard of the Carnegie Hall recording.

King Biscuit Flower Hour (also known as Live at the Royal Albert Hall with the Royal Philharmonic Orchestra, Part 1, as Greatest Hits Live, Part 1, and, with a different track order, as Can You Hear Me) (CD) and Novella (2019 Esoteric label reissue) (CD)

Originally released in February 1997, and subsequently repeatedly re-released under several different titles, and included as a bonus disc on the 2019 Esoteric label reissue of *Novella*, this is a recording of part of a 14 October 1977 concert with the Royal Philharmonic Orchestra at London's Royal Albert Hall. It was originally recorded for broadcast on a syndicated American radio program, *King Biscuit Flower Hour*, which at the time was carried by over 300 stations across the United States. Though only a portion of the concert was broadcast on the show, it has since been released in its entirety, distributed across two CDs, of which this is one.

The performances, by both band and orchestra, are excellent. However, while the sound quality is in most respects superior, it is slightly marred by persistent buzzes that evidently cannot be removed. (They are present even on the 2019 Esoteric release.) The buzzes are generally not perceptible during loud, or even medium-volume, passages, but one has to learn to ignore them during quiet ones.

King Biscuit Flower Hour, Vol. Two (also known as *Live at the Royal Albert Hall with the Royal Philharmonic Orchestra, Part 2*, as *Greatest Hits Live, Part 2*, and, with a different track order, as *Mother Russia*) (CD) and Novella (2019 Esoteric label reissue) **(CD).**
Originally released in March 1997, and, like its Part 1 companion, subsequently repeatedly re-released under several different titles, and included as a bonus disc on the 2019 Esoteric label reissue of *Novella*, this is a recording of the remainder of the 14 October 1977 concert, plus, in the case of the stand-alone CD, two additional tracks.

The buzzes remain.

One of the two bonus tracks on the stand-alone CD is a performance of 'Prologue' from a 28 January 1979 Asbury Park, New Jersey concert. The first pressing of the CD mistakenly contained a live recording of 'A Song for All Seasons' instead (even though the song was listed on the CD as 'Prologue'), but this was corrected in subsequent pressings. The other bonus track is a studio recording, 'You', which is also available on the *Songs From Renaissance Days* compilation album.

Dreams & Omens: 'Live' At The Tower Theatre, Philadelphia PA, 1978 (CD) **And A Song For All Seasons** (2019 Esoteric label reissue) **(CD)**

A 2008 release, *Dreams & Omens* collects, on one CD, six selections from a 4 December 1978 Philadelphia concert. It is superseded by the 2019 reissue of *A Song for All Seasons*, which includes those six tracks, plus four more (presumably the complete concert), on two CDs, in addition to three tracks recorded for BBC Radio One, and a studio recording of 'Northern Lights' for the *Top of the Pops* television show. The sound quality of the concert as it appears on the reissue is very good, and a substantial improvement over *Dreams & Omens*, which, while still quite enjoyable, is slightly distorted and a bit too trebly.

The three tracks recorded for BBC Radio One, on 19 August 1978, are 'Day of the Dreamer', 'Midas Man', and 'The Vultures Fly High'. These are fine performances, and good quality recordings, but, with the exception of the non-orchestral 'Day of the Dreamer', they stay very close to the original versions.

The same is true of the *Top Of The Pops* version of 'Northern Lights'. On that television program bands did not sing live, but rather mimed to a recording – not the actual released recording, but a copy, made especially for the show. Accordingly, this version sounds remarkably similar to the hit single, but there are a few, extremely minor, differences. Most notably, Sullivan's drum fill leading into the final round of repeated choruses is longer than the one on the official release, with the result that the *Top Of The Pops* version of the song is itself slightly longer than the hit version.

BBC Sessions (CD) And Live At The BBC: Sight & Sound (DVD/CD)

Released in 1999, the two-disc *BBC Sessions* album collects twelve tracks recorded for the BBC on four different dates: 8 May 1975, 25 March 1976, 6 January 1977 and 19 August 1978. It is superseded by *Live At The BBC: Sight & Sound*, which contains all of those, plus eight more, recorded on those same four dates, for a total of twenty tracks, spread across three CDs. This package also includes a DVD video of the 1977 session, a seven-song concert from London's Golders Green Hippodrome.

The complete programs for the 1976 and 1978 dates, included on *Live At The BBC*, are also available, respectively, on the 2019 reissues of *Live At Carnegie Hall* and *A Song For All Seasons*.

The 1975 session, recorded live in concert in London, includes, on both sets, an eighteen-minute rendition of 'Ashes Are Burning', and, on *Live At The BBC*, four additional tracks: 'Running Hard', 'Mother Russia', 'Prologue', and 'Ocean Gypsy', with these latter four orchestra-less performances sounding similar to the 1976 BBC versions.

But the highlight of the *Live At The BBC* set is the 1977 concert, which is presented on both CD and DVD – with the DVD containing the best available video of the classic-era Renaissance at its peak.

Day Of The Dreamer (CD)

A 2000 release, this one differs from other Renaissance live albums in that it is not a recording from one venue, but rather a collection of recordings made at different times and in different places. No information is provided as to when or where any of these performances took place. We are told that they all feature the classic line-up (Camp, Dunford, Haslam, Sullivan, and Tout), so at least we know that these are recordings of performances from the 1970s. Two of the CD's ten recordings are taken from the BBC albums. The remaining eight appear to be unique to this CD. The quality of the recordings is uniformly good. The same can be said for the quality of the performances.

Song Of Scheherazade: Renaissance Live (DVD)

A 2008 release, this DVD contains black and white footage from two New Jersey concerts, one from 1976, at the Capitol Theater in Passaic, and the other from 1979, at the Convention Centre in Asbury Park. These are non-orchestral concerts, featuring the classic 1970s line-up. While the audio quality is decent, the visuals are quite grainy, and, at times, blurry (with occasional ghosts, and deep shadows). It's a shame that the video quality is not better, as the performances are extraordinarily good.

135

Renaissance Filmed At Mill House And Bray Studios, 1979

Included as a bonus video on Scheherazade and Other Stories (2010 Friday Music label reissue) **(DVD)**

It is odd that this DVD, which contains videos of five Renaissance songs, would be attached to a reissue of *Scheherazade And Other Stories*, since none of the songs it includes are from that album, and all but one ('Carpet Of The Sun') are from *Azure D'Or*. Perhaps the explanation is that there is a market for reissues of the former album, but not for the latter.

Three of the videos, for 'Jekyll And Hyde', 'The Winter Tree', and 'Secret Mission', simply show the band in a studio miming to the relevant *Azure D'Or* track.

The other two, 'Forever Changing' and 'Carpet Of The Sun', are the only ones to feature new performances.

Live In Chicago (CD)

A 2010 release, this recording of a 1983 concert in Chicago's Park West venue is the only live Renaissance release from the *Time-Line* tour, and, with Tout and Sullivan now out of the band, the only one to feature Gavin Harrison (drums) and Mike Taylor (keyboards), alongside Camp, Dunford, and Haslam. The concert was originally recorded for a US television show, entitled *Hot Spots*, and the CD contains only the portion of it that was broadcast on that program. At roughly 41 minutes in length, this makes for a rather short live concert CD.

The back cover of the CD is highly deceptive, as it lists twelve tracks, many of them known to be lengthy, and does not list timings of individual songs, or indicate in any other way that the running time of the recording is barely over half that of a maxed-out CD.

So how is this possible? How could there be twelve Renaissance songs on a 41-minute recording? The answer is, there aren't. First, one of the listed songs, 'At the Harbour', does not appear on the recording at all. Secondly, seven of the remaining eleven are performed only in truncated form and run together as parts of a seventeen-and-a-half-minute medley. Finally, 'Running Hard' and 'Ashes Are Burning', while presented as stand-alone pieces, are nonetheless each reduced to seven minutes, with the famous piano introduction almost entirely excised from the former, and the latter actually beginning with the climactic 'Imagine the burning embers' section.

The sound quality of the CD is just fair – perfectly listenable, but with a certain amount of audible hiss and periodic distortion.

Unplugged: Live At The Academy Of Music, Philadelphia USA (CD)

A 2000 release, this is a recording of a 1985 concert, with Haslam and Dunford appearing as the only remaining members from the classic line-up (Camp having recently left the band). They are joined by recent recruits Raphael Rudd on piano and harp, Mark Lambert on guitar and bass, and Charles Descarfino on percussion. The CD is significant as the only release by this configuration of the band.

The sound of this quintet is different from that of all previous line-ups. Gone are the synthesizers, the electric guitar, and the rock-style drum kit. The emphasis is now on piano and acoustic guitar, plus the new sounds provided by Rudd's harp and Descarfino's varied assortment of orchestral percussion instruments.

The sound quality of the recording is reasonably good, although there is some noticeable distortion.

In The Land Of The Rising Sun (CD)

Released in 2002, this two-disc set captures a 16 March 2001 concert in Tokyo, from the band's brief 2001 tour of Japan in support of *Tuscany*. As such, it is a contemporary, rather than archival, live album – the band's first since *Live At Carnegie Hall*.

Terry Sullivan is back on drums for this one, joining Dunford and Haslam in a configuration featuring three-fifths of the classic 1970s line-up. Joining them are David Keyes, on bass, and two keyboardists – Mickey Simmonds and Rave Tesar. It is the only album to feature this lineup.

The sound quality is outstanding – clean and clear throughout, and with a good mix. The presence of two keyboard players, coupled with improvements in electronic keyboard technology and the skill of the players, allows the band to achieve a rich, full sound, including a reasonable simulation of orchestral parts. Unlike Renaissance's practice in the 1980s, here the songs are performed at their full length, and in arrangements that are reasonably faithful to the original studio recordings.

Tour 2011: Turn Of The Cards & Scheherazade And Other Stories – Live In Concert (DVD/CD)

Another contemporary, rather than archival, release, this is a recording, in both audio (2 CDs) and video formats, of a 23 September 2011 Glenside, Pennsylvania concert, in which the band plays all the pieces from two complete albums, *Turn Of The Cards* and *Scheherazade And Other Stories*, in their original running order, plus the song, 'The Mystic and the Muse'. The DVD also includes an interview with Haslam and Dunford.

The line-up, in addition to Haslam, Dunford, Tesar, and Keyes are two new recruits, drummer Frank Pagano, and (maintaining the two-keyboard approach established on *In The Land Of The Rising Sun*) Jason Hart. This is the only album to feature this configuration.

Haslam's voice is not quite the glorious instrument here that it was in the 1970s. At times one notices a lack of power at the end of a phrase, a tone that is less thick and rounded than it once was, and the occasional hint of a quaver. But her voice still holds up much better than most singers who have been at it as long as she has. And she still hits the high notes.

The sound quality is excellent. The video is fine for what it is – a straightforward, no fuss, look at the players as they play and sing these pieces.

Grandine Il Vento (Avalon label release) (CD)
Unlike the CD released in the US, this Japanese version, released the same year (2013), includes, as a bonus track, 'Carpet of the Sun', performed as a Haslam/Dunford acoustic duet.

Live At The Union Chapel (DVD, digital audio)
This ten-song, 90-minute concert performance was filmed live at the Union Chapel in London on 16 April 2015 and released the following year. Joining Haslam, Tesar, and Pagano in this version of the band are bassist Leo Traversa, keyboardist Tom Brislin (a *Grandine Il Vento* returnee), and, replacing Michael Dunford, who had died in November 2012, guitarist Mark Lambert (also in a return engagement, as he had been a band member in the mid-1980s). This is the only album to feature this lineup.

The quality of the audio, video, and performances is comparable to that of the *Tour 2011* presentation. The new material, especially 'Symphony of Light', and 'The Mystic and the Muse', holds its own in juxtaposition with the classics. The closer, 'Ashes Are Burning', is an eighteen-minute version, with lengthy solos in the middle by Tesar, on piano, Traversa, on bass, and Brislin, on synthesizer. Haslam performs her vocalise riffs in the coda and shows that she can still fly in the stratosphere.

A Symphonic Journey (DVD/CD)
Released in 2018, this recording, in both audio and video formats, is of a 27 October 2017 concert in Glenside, Pennsylvania – the same venue at which the band had performed for its *Tour 2011* audio/video album. This time, however, Renaissance plays with a small orchestra, their very own ten-piece 'Renaissance Chamber Orchestra', consisting of a string quartet, a percussionist, and five wind and brass players (covering flute, clarinet, oboe, English horn, trumpet, flugelhorn, French horn, and trombone). The last time the band had played in concert with an orchestra had been in 1977, forty years previously.

Joining Haslam, Lambert, Tesar, and Traversa, in this version of Renaissance, are newcomer Geoffrey Langley, on keyboards, and returnee Charles Descarfino (who, like Lambert, had been in the mid-1980s band), on drums and percussion. This is the only album to feature this configuration.

Two special features of the DVD are noteworthy. First, Haslam, an accomplished abstract and semi-abstract painter, had made, for the occasion, several very colourful paintings – one for each of the songs performed at the concert. Enlarged projections of them appear on a screen behind the musicians as they play – a bonus visual treat in the concert video.

The DVD also includes an interesting and informative 30-minute 'Behind the Scenes' documentary, featuring rehearsal footage, interspersed with brief interviews with the members of the orchestra.

Compilation Albums

While there are many Renaissance compilation albums, most of them are simply collections of previously released tracks. With one exception, the discussions in this chapter only concern compilations that go beyond what is available on other studio or live albums. All of the 'previously unreleased' songs contained in these releases are discussed above as 'Related Tracks' in connection with the album to which they are most closely connected.

Innocents And Illusions

A two-CD set released in 2004, this is a reissue of the first two studio albums, *Renaissance* and *Illusion*. It contains the following bonus tracks: 'The Sea', 'Shining Where The Sun Has Been', 'All The Fallen Angels', 'Prayer For Light', and 'Walking Away'.

Songs From Renaissance Days

A 1997 release, this single-disc set collects demos and other unreleased recordings, plus one non-album B-side, all drawn from the 1979-1988 period.

Da Capo

This 1995 release is a two-CD career retrospective, representing every studio album released in the 1969-1983 period, plus two previously unreleased tracks. While this collection provides an excellent overview of the band's career during the years in question, it doesn't really function as a 'best of' album, primarily because the inclusion of seven tracks from the band's comparatively weak 1979-1983 period crowds out much stronger earlier material that might have been included instead.

Tales of 1001 Nights, Volume One and Tales of 1001 Nights, Volume Two

While these two single-disc compilations are packaged and sold separately, they are clearly two parts of a single project, and thus are discussed together here. Released on CD in 1990, when none of the band's albums were yet available in that format, these collections have sold very well with no promotion or marketing campaign.

Presumably in order to avoid licensing fees, all of the selections are drawn from the band's 1974-1979 recordings (*Turn Of The Cards* to *Azure D'Or*), as these were all made for the same label. Happily, this coincides with the band's best period, especially when taking into account the fact that two fine earlier albums, *Prologue* and *Ashes Are Burning*, are also indirectly represented, in that songs initially on them are here included by means of good live versions from the *Live At Carnegie Hall* album.

Within these constraints, the compilers made excellent choices, focusing primarily on the proggy epics, so that the two discs, taken together, make for a superior 'best of' album, and an outstanding listening experience. In this respect, this collection is far superior to *Da Capo*. But on the other hand, because it excludes the pre-Haslam era, as well as the 1980s material, it is inferior to *Da Capo* as a representation of the band's history.

Solo Albums And Other Related Recordings

It would be impossible, and pointless, to discuss every recording that every one-time member of Renaissance has made as a solo artist or as a member of another band. For example, although John Wetton was the Renaissance bass player for a few months in 1970 and 1971, his subsequent brilliant career in King Crimson, UK, Asia, and as a solo artist is, at best, of marginal significance to the Renaissance story. Thus, this chapter focuses only on recordings that are fairly closely connected to those that Renaissance itself has made.

Keith Relf: All The Falling Angels: Solo Recordings & Collaborations 1965–1976

A 2020 release, this 24-track collection includes five tracks Relf made with Jim McCarty in 1968 under the name 'Together', the duo that evolved the next year into the first incarnation of Renaissance. Among these five songs are 'Henry's Coming Home' and 'Love Mum and Dad', both sides of the one single that the pair released before adding three players, thus becoming Renaissance.

Jane Relf: Jane's Renaissance: The Complete Jane Relf Collection, 1969-1995

A two-CD, 33-track compilation, this 2009 release collects recordings throughout her career (including with Renaissance). Demos, B-sides, previously unreleased work, and rarities are included. Of special interest is her demo recording of 'Carpet of the Sun', which would later become a Haslam-era Renaissance classic.

Shoot: On The Frontier (1973)

Originally released on LP, but subsequently issued on CD, this is the sole album put out by this Jim McCarty-led quartet (he was the band's lead vocalist and principal songwriter). John Tout plays on one song. The title track, a McCarty/Thatcher composition, is covered by Renaissance on *Ashes Are Burning*.

Illusion: Out Of The Mist (1977), Illusion (1978), And Enchanted Caress (1990)

Four-fifths of the original Renaissance (Jim McCarty, Jane Relf, Louis Cennamo, and John Hawken, thus missing only the recently deceased Keith Relf) reunited under the name 'Illusion' to make these recordings. While the first album charted in the US, the follow-up did not sell, and the band was dropped by their label. Both of these albums have since been released on CD.

Enchanted Caress, released on CD in 1990, is a collection of demos that the band recorded in 1979, in an effort to attract record company interest in a third album by the group. Unable to find a label willing to participate in such a project, Illusion split up, and the songs remained in demo form.

Renaissance Illusion: Through The Fire (2001)

In 2001, McCarty, Cenammo, Hawken, and Jane Relf once again reunited to record this album of new material, under the name 'Renaissance Illusion'. A 2017 CD reissue contains two bonus tracks.

Nevada: Pictures In The Fire (2000)

Following the disappointing sales of the 1979 album, *Azure d'Or*, Renaissance was dropped by its label. When John Tout and Terry Sullivan left the band the next year, it appeared that there would be no more Renaissance. Annie Haslam and Michael Dunford then teamed up with keyboardist Peter Gosling (who would subsequently play on *Camera Camera* and *Time-Line*) to form a new, three-piece, band, Nevada.

This group released a single in 1980, 'In The Bleak Midwinter', backed with 'Pictures In The Fire'. It made a minor dent on the UK singles chart, reaching number 71. Nevada released one more single, 1981's 'You Know I Like It', backed with 'Once In A Lifetime'. It failed to chart, and the band released nothing else, as Renaissance reunited that year to make *Camera Camera*. However, Nevada did record several demos, and these are collected on this CD, released in 2000. It is an extremely poor quality CD, as the demos are all derived from secondary sources, the result of the original tapes having been either lost or destroyed. Moreover, the four songs from the two released singles are represented here by inferior alternate recordings, not the released versions.

Annie Haslam: Annie In Wonderland (1977), Still Life (1985), Annie Haslam (1989), Live Under Brazilian Skies (1998), The Dawn Of Ananda (1999), It Snows In Heaven Too (2000), One Enchanted Evening (2002), Live Studio Concert (2006), Woman Transcending (2007)

Annie Haslam has made nine solo albums over the years, mostly during times of inactivity by Renaissance.

Annie In Wonderland, made between *Novella* and *A Song For All Seasons*, when a brief John Tout illness brought about a break in Renaissance's schedule, gave her a chance to explore styles outside the scope of her band. Two of the songs on the album are Jon Camp compositions, and Camp also plays on four tracks. The album charted in the US at 167. The 2010 remastered CD contains a newly-recorded bonus track.

Still Life, recorded with Louis Clark and the Royal Philharmonic Orchestra, consists of popular classical melodies, by the likes of Tchaikovsky, J. S. Bach, Mozart, Chopin, and Wagner, set to lyrics by chief Renaissance lyricist, Betty Thatcher, played by the orchestra, and sung by Haslam. Interestingly, Thatcher and Haslam decided here to take a second crack at Remo Giazotto's 1958 composition, *Adagio In G minor For Strings And Organ*, which Thatcher and Renaissance had turned into 'Cold is Being' on *Turn Of The Cards*. Here

Thatcher and Haslam turn it into 'Save Us All'.

Annie Haslam, a more pop-oriented album, includes 'The Angels Cry', written by Justin Hayward of the Moody Blues. Hayward also plays and sings on the track.

Live Under Brazilian Skies is a sixteen-track concert recording, in which Haslam sings several Renaissance songs, in addition to songs from her solo albums. Also noteworthy is a beautiful rendition of a classic song by Yes, 'Turn of the Century', which she had previously recorded on *Tales From Yesterday*, a Yes tribute album.

The Dawn Of Ananda, an album with a theme (angels), contains mostly original songs, with lyrics by Haslam, and music by the likes of Michael Dunford, Rave Tesar, and Tony Visconti, among others.

It Snows In Heaven Too is a 16-track Christmas album, full of such standards as 'Silent Night', 'Joy to the World', 'We Three Kings', 'The Little Drummer Boy', 'Away in a Manger', and 'White Christmas'.

One Enchanted Evening is a recording of a 23 June 2001 concert given in Upper Black Eddy, Pennsylvania. The program consists of old classics, many of them show tunes. The concert closer is 'She's Leaving Home', from the Beatles' *Sgt. Pepper's Lonely Hearts Club Band* album.

Live Studio Concert, released in both CD and DVD formats, is a recording of a ten-track 1997 Philadelphia studio concert. The program is varied, but includes the Renaissance songs 'Carpet of the Sun', 'The Captive Heart', and 'The Young Prince and Princess as Told by Scheherazade'.

Woman Transcending is a sixteen-track compilation featuring rare and previously unreleased pieces recorded for a variety of projects over the years.

Haslam has also been featured on a number of tribute albums, singing songs by other famous artists. Examples, in addition to the already-mentioned Yes tribute album, are 'Ripples', on the Genesis tribute album, *Supper's Ready*, and 'It's All Over Now, Baby Blue', on Yes guitarist Steve Howe's 1999 *Portraits of Bob Dylan* album. The latter song is significant in that it had previously been sung by Joan Baez, a singer whom Haslam reports having idolised and emulated when she was young.

Annie Haslam's Renaissance: Blessing in Disguise (1994)

Haslam explains that when she was ready to make a follow-up to her 1989 solo album, *Annie Haslam*, her fans kept telling her that she should use the name 'Renaissance', so that 'people know who you are'. So she called it 'Annie Haslam's Renaissance' for one album, but subsequently thought better of it, and went back to 'The Annie Haslam Band'.

Having previously worked almost exclusively as a singer of material written by others, Haslam began, with this project, to participate significantly in the songwriting process, writing lyrics to nine songs on the album. The album's producer, Tony Visconti, perhaps best known for his work with David Bowie, also contributes several compositions to the album, setting Haslam's lyrics to music.

The 2005 reissue contains two bonus tracks, both recorded in 2002.

Michael Dunford's Renaissance: The Other Woman (1995) and Ocean Gypsy (1997)

Michael Dunford's major project, following the 1987 breakup of Renaissance, was an attempt to create a theatrical production based on 'The Song of Scheherazade', the epic piece that had filled side two of Renaissance's 1975 album, *Scheherazade And Other Stories*. In that connection, he met Stephanie Adlington, a young American singer. The two decided to make an album together, and Dunford, noting that Annie Haslam had used the Renaissance name for her *Blessing In Disguise* album of the previous year, decided that he might do so as well. Thus, in 1995 'Michael Dunford's Renaissance' co-existed with 'Annie Haslam's Renaissance' – two completely different bands.

All of the songs are by the classic Renaissance songwriting ream of Dunford and Betty Thatcher (now Newsinger), and most of them are new, though a remake of 'Northern Lights' is included. Dunford, speaking in 1995, the year of this album's release, explains why the new material doesn't sound much like that of the classic-era Renaissance: 'I think nowadays you can't have tracks that are too long. Music evolves, obviously, and in the 70s that was the time for those sorts of tracks, but now ... It doesn't have to be three minutes long, it can be double that length of time, but nothing gets too involved. I think the attention span can't take it anymore'.

Dunford subsequently expressed dissatisfaction with the album, feeling that it had turned out as too much of a rock album.

Ocean Gypsy, which again features Adlington as lead vocalist, differs from its predecessor in that it contains only two new songs, with the remaining seven tracks being remakes of Renaissance classics, all of them originally released in the 1973-1975 period, and all drawn from just three albums: *Ashes Are Burning*, *Turn Of The Cards*, and *Scheherazade And Other Stories*. Unlike the remake of 'Northern Lights' on *The Other Woman*, here Dunford at least offers new arrangements of these old, familiar songs. In some cases, flutes, saxes, and/or synthesized strings are used on pieces that previously lacked them. In other cases, tracks that had featured rich orchestration are now offered in more stripped-down arrangements. In still others, where a drum kit might have been used on the original recording, different percussion instruments are now used instead. The album also differs from its immediate predecessor in that it is, for the most part, an acoustic production, with fewer rock elements.

Renaissant: South Of Winter (2004)

This is basically a Terry Sullivan project, as he composed the music for it, and, as a performer, plays drums, keyboards, and guitar, and, on two of the album's nine tracks, sings lead. He gets help from some of his Renaissance associates, as John Tout plays keyboards, and Betty Newsinger (formerly Thatcher) contributes lyrics.